797,885 Books

are available to read at

www.ForgottenBooks.com

Forgotten Books' App
Available for mobile, tablet & eReader

ISBN 978-1-330-88635-9
PIBN 10117159

This book is a reproduction of an important historical work. Forgotten Books uses state-of-the-art technology to digitally reconstruct the work, preserving the original format whilst repairing imperfections present in the aged copy. In rare cases, an imperfection in the original, such as a blemish or missing page, may be replicated in our edition. We do, however, repair the vast majority of imperfections successfully; any imperfections that remain are intentionally left to preserve the state of such historical works.

Forgotten Books is a registered trademark of FB &c Ltd.
Copyright © 2015 FB &c Ltd.
FB &c Ltd, Dalton House, 60 Windsor Avenue, London, SW19 2RR.
Company number 08720141. Registered in England and Wales.

For support please visit www.forgottenbooks.com

1 MONTH OF
FREE
READING

at

www.ForgottenBooks.com

By purchasing this book you are eligible for one month membership to ForgottenBooks.com, giving you unlimited access to our entire collection of over 700,000 titles via our web site and mobile apps.

To claim your free month visit: www.forgottenbooks.com/free117159

* Offer is valid for 45 days from date of purchase. Terms and conditions apply.

English
Français
Deutsche
Italiano
Español
Português

www.forgottenbooks.com

Mythology Photography **Fiction**
Fishing Christianity **Art** Cooking
Essays Buddhism Freemasonry
Medicine **Biology** Music **Ancient
Egypt** Evolution Carpentry Physics
Dance Geology **Mathematics** Fitness
Shakespeare **Folklore** Yoga Marketing
Confidence Immortality Biographies
Poetry **Psychology** Witchcraft
Electronics Chemistry History **Law**
Accounting **Philosophy** Anthropology
Alchemy Drama Quantum Mechanics
Atheism Sexual Health **Ancient History**
Entrepreneurship Languages Sport
Paleontology Needlework Islam
Metaphysics Investment Archaeology
Parenting Statistics Criminology
Motivational

HURD'S

LETTERS ON CHIVALR

AND ROMANCE

WITH THE

THIRD ELIZABETHAN DIALOGUE

EDITED WITH INTRODUCTION

BY

EDITH J. MORLEY

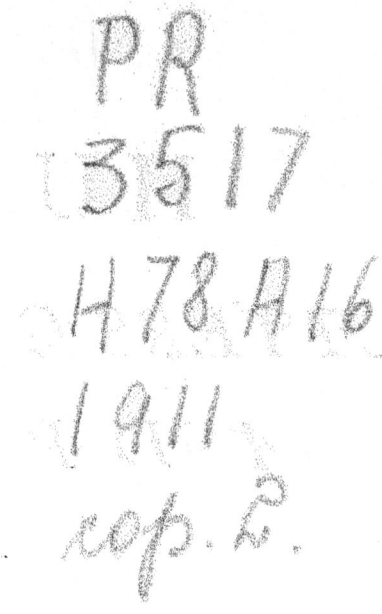

PR
3517
H78 A16
1911
cop. 2.

OXFORD : HORACE HART
PRINTER TO THE UNIVERSITY

PREFACE.

HURD's *Letters on Chivalry and Romance* have been curiously neglected, considering how strong a light they throw upon the trend of critical thought in the second half of the eighteenth century. There has been no separate reprint for more than a century, while the only complete collected edition of his Works appeared as long ago as 1811.

It is hoped that this edition of the *Third Dialogue* and of the *Letters on Chivalry and Romance* may help to reinstate Hurd in his rightful position among the heralds of the romantic revival in criticism. The text of the *Letters* has been reprinted from the first edition, which appeared in 1762, and has been carefully collated with that of the last edition which appeared during the author's lifetime, namely, that of 1788. The variations, other than those which are merely typographical, or unimportant changes in spelling and punctuation, are given in footnotes and appendices, and many of them show clearly the advance that was made in Hurd's critical outlook between these dates. The Dialogue, the authorship of which Hurd did not acknowledge when it first appeared, attributing it in a footnote to the Hon. Robt. Digby, has been reprinted from the edition of 1788.

The following is a list of the editions of *Letters on Chivalry and Romance* and *Moral and Political Dialogues*:

Letters on Chivalry and Romance, 1762 (reprinted in the same year).

Moral and Political Dialogues, 1759 (reprinted in 1760).

Moral and Political Dialogues, with Letters on Chivalry and Romance, 1765 (reprinted in 1771, 1776, and 1788).

Works of Richard Hurd, complete edition, 1811.

Apart from Hurd's own works, and his list of the chief occurrences in his life which is included in this volume, the following are the most important books which refer to him and his achievements :—

Kilvert : *Life of Hurd.*
Cradock : *Literary Memoirs.*
Dictionary of National Biography.
Chalmers : *Biographical Dictionary.*
Nichols : *Literary Anecdotes.*
Mme. d'Arblay : *Diary.*
Walpole : *Letters.*
Lessing : *Hamburgische Dramaturgie.*
Leslie Stephen : *English Thought in the Eighteenth Century.*
Saintsbury : *History of Criticism.*
Beers : *Romanticism in the Eighteenth Century.*
Phelps : *The Beginnings of the English Romantic Movement.*
Gosse : *Eighteenth Century Literature.*
Seccombe : *The Age of Johnson.*
Hamelius : *Die Kritik in der englischen Literatur des 17. und 18. Jahrhunderts.*

In conclusion, I wish to express my sincere gratitude to Professor Ker and to Miss M. L. Lee for their kindness in reading the MS. of my Introduction, and for the helpful suggestions they were good enough to make.

EDITH J. MORLEY.

UNIVERSITY COLLEGE, READING.
October, 1911.

CONTENTS.

INTRODUCTION.

'THE ages, we call barbarous, present us with many a subject of curious speculation.' These words, with which Hurd opens his *Letters on Chivalry and Romance*, written in 1762, are epoch-making, in that they offer to eighteenth-century critics and scholars a new and hitherto undreamed-of point of view. The orthodox believers in classical rules and Aristotelian laws, the upholders of the 'Kinds' and those who pinned their faith to sanity, clearness, and common sense, were accustomed to dismiss the Middle Ages contemptuously as barbarous times, unworthy of serious investigation and discussion. The Augustan Age was not easily impressed by that spirit of mystery and wonder which is one of the attractions of mediaeval romance. Even Dryden regrets that Spenser did not know the maxims of Bossu ; most critics agree that Shakespeare suffered from his lack of art ; Milton is praised by Addison himself rather for the successful conduct of the war in heaven than for the romantic adventures of Satan in the infinities of space.

Eighteenth-century classicists were not, as a rule, attracted to tales of gramarye : they were not prepared to yield, even momentarily, that 'suspension of disbelief which constitutes poetic faith ', nor had they even a dim perception of the truth that

> '. . . nothing worthy proving can be proven,
>   Nor yet disproven '.

Yet in the very midst of the age of reason and of law the reaction began, and manifested itself in a multiplicity of ways. 'The return to nature,' the 'romantic revival,' 'the renascence of wonder,' call it by whatever name we choose, was not a sudden and unexpected phenomenon. The *Lyrical Ballads* of 1798 were by no means the first indication of the change which was taking place in prevalent habits of thought and modes of expression. In criticism, men of letters early began, almost in spite of themselves, to reject the gods to whom they still professed allegiance. The citadel of classicism was first assaulted by the friends who claimed to defend it, and the attack was so insidious as to be irresistible. The very men who do most to bring about the Romantic Revival are strangely averse to its spirit of freedom and of individuality. Richard Hurd, the neo-classic upholder of Pope, the defender of *Poetical Imitation*, is one of the earliest to deviate from the beaten track, and is consequently of more importance than the ordinary neglect of his writings would lead one to suppose. In his own day, indeed, he was generally admired and esteemed[1]; welcomed by the royal family at Windsor and elsewhere, as Fanny Burney faithfully records in her *Diary*; a visitor to the Literary Club, where Dr. Johnson at any rate thought him worthy of his powder and shot; the correspondent of Gray and some of his friends; the intimate of Pope's champion, Warburton. It is perhaps this last alliance which has helped to bring him into disrepute. Macaulay's inscription in a copy of the *Letters from a late eminent prelate to one of his friends,* summed up their correspondence as that of 'Bully to Sneak'. The latter title is not merited by Hurd, who, with all his formal conventionalism

---

[1] Professor Phelps, in *The Beginnings of the English Romantic Movement* (New York, 1893), says, 'Hurd's learning and authoritative position counted for much' in making his influence widely felt among critics and readers of poetry.

and love of show and ceremony, appears fairly to have earned his position as Bishop of Worcester by his learning as well as by his careful observance of clerical duties. But Dr. Johnson would probably have been right had he called Hurd as he called 'Hermes Harris', 'a prig, and a bad prig,' and such men are not as a rule attractive personalities. Even as a man, however, he does not deserve the harsh strictures of Sir Leslie Stephen (*English Thought in the Eighteenth Century*, vol. I, vii, 4 and 5), and as a critic he is incomparably greater than Mr. Edmund Gosse (*Eighteenth Century Literature*, p. 395) would seem to imply.

Hurd has written enough to show that he possessed real scholarship and critical acumen. But his editions of Horace and of Addison, and his various *Critical Dissertations*, though they prove his learning, do not secure his fame. In 1759 there appeared his *Moral and Political Dialogues*, the third and fourth of which deal with the age of Queen Elizabeth. The speakers are Digby, Arbuthnot, and Addison, whose visit to Kenilworth causes them to converse about 'the princely shows and sports which were once so proudly celebrated within these walls'.[1] Addison is reminded of nothing but 'barbarous manners and a despotic government', while Arbuthnot defends past times, and goes so far as to say that 'Gothic tilts and tournaments exceeded, both in use and elegance, even the Græcian gymnastics'. This comparison is characteristic of Hurd's standpoint, which is also that of all those in whom the 'antiquarian spirit' is in any way aroused. One of the most striking signs of the times is this revival and discovery of history—the newly awakened imaginative interest in the past, not as a mine from which examples and comparisons may be digged, but as a source of information concerning the rock from which we have been hewn. Gibbon's *Decline and Fall* (1776) is the first great work in which the differences between the centuries are made apparent, and his *Essay upon the Study of Literature* (1761) (written in French) is one of the earliest attempts to deal with the development of literature. Thomas Warton's *History of English Poetry* (1774–81) is a much more ambitious venture in the same direction. He writes it in order to trace 'the dawnings of genius and to pursue the progress of our national poetry from a rude origin and obscure beginnings'.

Realization of growth and development from century to century naturally goes hand in hand with a wider interest in, and sympathy for, the life and aims of past ages, a breaking down of barriers and an appeal to a less circumscribed experience. This accounts for the attempts to understand Shakespeare or Spenser and their respective points of view—to judge them with reference to Elizabethan times and Elizabethan ideals, not by an appeal to a standard which was unrecognized when they wrote. Hurd's *Dialogues on the Age of Queen Elizabeth* unites both these tendencies. He is immensely interested in the study of history : he has no hide-bound views about the pre-eminence of any particular period ; for his part he considers 'the legends of chivalry in a very serious light', and he does not scruple to praise Pindar and Homer himself as 'ancient masters of romance'. Perhaps most important of all is the stress he lays on the value of early writings as a true representation of the life and ideas of past ages, without some knowledge of which they cannot therefore be judged. In the *Letters on Chivalry and Romance*, as we shall see, this opinion is further developed into the express statement that there are different types of poetry, each of which must be criticized according to its own aims and ends.

This recognition of the existence of two distinct schools, the Gothic and the Classic, and Hurd's acceptance of both as worthy of admiration, leads him to make the comparison which forms the most valuable part of the *Letters on Chivalry and Romance*. We shall best appreciate it by summarizing his main argument and conclusions.

The first Letter justifies Johnson's criticism of Hurd, as belonging to a 'set of men who account for everything systematically'. In it he not only proclaims the inherent interest of Gothic chivalry and the spirit of Romance, but sets out to discover 'some latent cause of their production', and the conditions and circumstances in which they had their origin. For, since some of the greatest geniuses of our own and foreign countries, Ariosto, Tasso, Spenser, Milton, have been charmed by old romances, there may possibly be something in them 'peculiarly suited to the views of a genius, and to the ends of poetry'. He proceeds therefore to a study of 'the rise, progress, and genius of Gothic chivalry', and of the reasons 'for the decline and rejection of Gothic taste in later times'. In Letter II he gives the historical facts upon which he bases his opinion that chivalry was 'the natural and even sober effect of the feudal policy', for the characteristics of which (Letter III) it is consequently easy to account. 'Prowess, Generosity, Gallantry, and Religion' are the natural virtues of a military age. In the next Letter,

information, stating in so many words that he has not perused the ' barbarous ' old Romances himself. As a classical scholar he has no personal leanings to this ' ungrateful task '— a curious sidelight on his attitude of mind. It is in this same Letter IV that Hurd begins his comparison of the ' circumstances of agreement between the *heroic* and *gothic* manners ', which implies the most remarkable admission in the book. The recognition of the correspondence between the manners of the old heroic times, ' as painted by their great romancer Homer,[1] and those which are represented to us in the books of modern knight errantry,' tacitly accepts the premise which is later on amplified, that comparison between the two ages is natural and justifiable. This is a long step towards the admission of possible equality in other matters. Thus criticism has by this time enlarged its boundaries : it is no longer solely occupied with preconceived literary theories, treated invariably from the same point of view. It is beginning to include in its scope, the life of the individual and of the nation to which he belongs ; to demand the investigation of philosophical and social questions ; to study literary history, and simultaneously the history of thought and of life. The new test of the value of a work is coming slowly to be its relationship with other things.

Hurd works out in some detail the resemblances between the political conditions of ancient Greece and those of feudal times, concluding (Letter V) that the poets of each age will, as a result of this likeness, be engaged in the representation of similar subjects. 'So far as the heroic and Gothic manners are the same, the pictures of each, if well taken, must be equally entertaining' (Letter VI). Nay, further, the advantage is clearly with the age of chivalry, because of 'the improved gallantry of the feudal times, and the superior solemnity of their superstitions'. It is a far cry from the Augustan contempt for Gothic rudeness to the admission that 'the mummeries of the pagan priests were childish, but the Gothic Enchanters shook and alarmed all nature. We feel this difference very sensibly in reading the ancient and modern poets. You would not compare the *Canidia* of Horace with the Witches in *Macbeth*. And what are Virgil's myrtles dropping blood, to Tasso's enchanted forest ? ' After this, even the conclusion of the Letter, with its bold claim for romantic poetry, ceases to be altogether overwhelming : 'We are upon enchanted ground, my friend ; and you are to think yourself well used that I detain you no longer in this fearful circle. The glympse you have had of it will help your imagination to conceive the rest. And without more words you will readily apprehend that the fancies of our modern bards are not only more gallant, but, on a change of the scene, more sublime, more terrible, more alarming, than those of the classic fablers. In a word, you will find that the *manners* they paint, and the *superstitions* they adopt, are the more poetical for being Gothic.'

Evidently 'the charms of *fairy* prevailed' with Hurd ; in spite of his classical bias, he had, like his betters, 'a certain predilection for—

> '. . . forests and enchantments drear,
> Where more is meant than meets the ear.'

In Letter VII he shows that Spenser and Milton, the English poets who best merit comparison with Homer, were both 'rapt with the Gothic fables of chivalry'. Thus Spenser, who might 'no doubt' have planned a poem on the classic model, deliberately chose the Gothic, and it is as a Gothic poem that the *Faerie Queen* is to be read and criticized—another specific statement that literature must be judged 'with the same spirit that the author writ', irrespective of current standards.

Milton, though he preferred the classic model, hesitated long as to his choice of subject, and even though he determined against 'Arthur and his Knights of the round table', 'we see thro' all his poetry, where his enthusiasm flames out most', a genuine delight in the legends of chivalry. Clearly, it is no defect in Hurd's eyes, that Milton gives way to 'enthusiasm': the implication appears rather to be that he is at such moments greatest. The appeal to Spenser and Milton serves, in itself, as a forcible reminder how greatly the good bishop was influenced by the Warton brothers. On the whole, Hurd's views are more advanced and better supported than those of the first edition of Thomas Warton's *Observations on the Faerie Queen* [1] (1754). But the line of argument is very similar, and Warton has the advantage of earlier publication to counterbalance his obvious self-restraint in expression.

[1] The second edition, which appeared in the same year as Hurd's *Letters*, is much more emphatic about the need to study the age of chivalry in all its bearings. Old romances throw considerable light on the nature of the feudal system. 'Above all, such are their Terrible Graces of magic and enchantment, so magnificently marvellous are their fictions and fablings, that they contribute in a wonderful degree to rouse and invigorate all the powers of the imagination: to store the fancy with those sublime and alarming images, which true poetry best delights to display' (vide Postscriptum).

Hurd's seventh Letter concludes with the explicit statement that Shakespeare is at his best when he uses Gothic
manners and machinery, and that this may be taken as
a further proof of their superiority to the classical 'in producing the sublime'. Letter VIII is in some respects the
most important of the whole series. It emphasizes the
earlier contention that a poem must be judged according
to the ideal which the poet has set before himself, since 'when
an architect examines a Gothic structure by Grecian rules,
he finds nothing but deformity. But the Gothic architecture
has it's own rules, by which, when it comes to be examined,
it is seen to have it's merit, as well as the Grecian. The
question is not which of the two is constructed in the simplest or truest taste : but, whether there be not sense and
design in both, when scrutinized by the laws on which each
is projected.' Hurd goes on to prove his capacity to deal
with his subject, by an examination of the *Faerie Queene* in
the light of this belief. He goes further, indeed, than most
modern critics, when he maintains that it has 'that sort of
unity and simplicity which results from it's nature '. On the
other hand, there is real critical acumen in the realization
that the 'classic ideas of Unity . . . have no place here '.
Hurd is firm in his conviction that pedantic faith in the rules
can only mislead the admirers of Spenser. The representation
of one entire action is not the only possible unity. Spenser
has achieved 'unity of design ', which is sufficient to knit
the poem together and make it, as Aristotle demands, 'serious,
complete, and of a certain magnitude.' Spenser goes wrong
only when he allows his knowledge of the classic rules to cause
him to confuse two different kinds of composition. It was
a vain attempt to achieve unity of action by giving 'the

introducing ' one superior character which should be seen throughout '. ' His expedients were injudicious. Their purpose was to ally two things, in nature incompatible, the Gothic, and the classic unity ; . . . I am of opinion . . . the Poet had done well to affect no other unity than that of *design,* by which his subject was connected.'

For a similar reason, i. e. that Spenser was mistaken in attempting to blend two different kinds of writing, Hurd objects to the allegory, though he admits that this justifies, for its own purpose, the introduction of Prince Arthur. The moral is needed to give unity to an allegorical poem : the ideas and usages of chivalry give unity of design to the narrative. But ' from the union of the two designs there arises a perplexity and confusion, which is the proper, and only considerable, defect of this extraordinary poem '.

The wisdom of Spenser's determination to make the form of his work correspond with his subject is shown by a comparison between the *Faerie Queen* and the *Gierusalemme Liberata* (Letter IX). Tasso conducts his fable with strict regard to the unity of action, but Hurd obviously considers Spenser's plan to be far more successful, even though French critics had formerly been loud in their praises of Tasso— apart from ' his magic tales and faery enchantments '. But though Tasso is preferred to Ariosto by the French criticism which superseded Italian taste, ' the mixture of the Gothic manner in his work has not been forgiven.' English imitators blindly follow French authority, and the ' Gothic manner ' becomes the favourite object of raillery with Davenant, Rymer, ' and the rest of that school ', including Lord Shaftes- bury. Finally, ' cold Boileau happened to say something of the *clinquant* of Tasso,' and Italian poetry-at once stood condemned in the eyes of all pretenders to taste, and even of

Addison himself. The greatest English critics (Letter X) condemn Italian poets, in spite of their manifest beauties. This is because they hold that tales of faery are unnatural and absurd, and that, moreover, the poets 'expect to have their lyes believed'. Hurd's answer is significant. 'They think it enough, if they can but bring you to *imagine* the possibility of them.' This looks like the foreshadowing of Coleridge's defence of supernatural subjects, and of the romantic belief in the worth of imagination and of imaginative conceptions.[1] 'So little account does this wicked poetry make of philosophical or historical truth : All she allows us to look for, is *poetical truth*,' and this is not limited to 'the conceived possibility of nature'. Hurd enlarges upon this dictum, which he quotes from Hobbes. To follow nature is not to be confined to 'the known and experienced course of affairs in this world'. In the poet's realm, imagination is of more importance than experience : 'all is marvellous and extraordinary,' though not necessarily in every sense 'unnatural'. In those species of poetry which professedly deal with men and manners, or with human passions, the laws of probability must be strictly observed if the reader is to be moved and affected. 'But the case is different with the more sublime and creative poetry' which addresses itself 'solely or principally to the Imagination'. [It should be remembered that the poetry most in vogue when Hurd was writing does not come into this category as here defined.] 'The *divine dream* and delirious fancy are among the noblest of' poetic prerogatives ; the resulting 'fictions' are undervalued only because 'readers do not usually do, as they ought, put themselves in the circumstance of the poet, or rather of those of whom the

poet writes.' Here Hurd is emphatically on the side of the
angels—or at any rate of modern critical aesthetics, as contrasted with the more limited conceptions of his own century.

Letter XI is in some ways more commonplace in subject-
matter than its predecessors. It examines the reasons why
'classical manners are still admired and imitated by the
poets when the Gothic have long since fallen into disuse.' But
Hurd's treatment of the question is refreshingly novel. He
points out that no great poet arose to do honour to Gothic
manners, while very early real genius, in the person of
Chaucer, was employed against them. *Sir Thopas* laughs at
the exaggerations of the old romances, which, with their
extravagant pictures, were already out of date. According to
Hurd, who is not an authority on the subject, Chaucer exposes
their 'impertinencies only '—the abuses of the 'phantoms of
chivalry', not its fair representation by a capable writer; but
then no such writer arose until the manners which sprang
out of the feudal system appeared unnatural, because anti-
quated and superseded. Thus 'romance', because suited
only to an artificial code of etiquette peculiar to a particular
age, has become a term of contempt, 'while the classic manners,
as arising out of the customary and usual situations of
humanity,' remain eternally fresh and natural. Spenser
must, therefore, for aught Hurd can see, 'be left to the
admiration of a few lettered and curious men' who know
enough of the 'barbarous ages' to believe that 'romantic
manners' ever really existed.

The last Letter (XII) attempts to trace the gradual revolution in modern taste which led to the rejection of the
wonders of chivalry and of romance. Ultimately reason gained
'the ascendant over the portentous spectres of the imagination. It's growing splendour, in the end, put them all to

and allowed them no quarter even amongst the poets '.
non sense was offended by the perversion of truth ;
:y, that had wantoned it so long in the world of fiction,
now constrained, against her will, to ally herself with
truth if she would gain admittance into reasonable
any. What we have gotten by this revolution, you will
a great deal of good sense. What we have lost, is a world
e fabling ; the illusion of which is so grateful to the
ned spirit.'

this note Hurd ends his Letters. He did not die (1808)
a fresh revolution of taste—of which he is a herald—
een completed. There is, alas, no record to tell us how
eeted *The Ancient Mariner* and [1] *Christabel* : we do not
know whether he read *The Lay of the Last Minstrel.*
Letters on Chivalry and Romance incline one to believe
iticism would have been more just than that of *Quarterly*
Edinburgh reviewers, more discriminating than that of
n, with his talk about 'stale romance '.

The following particulars, in the author's own hand-
ng, and endorsed by him—"Some Occurrences in my
R.W."—were found amongst his papers after his
ise.'

hristabel was not published until 1816, but it was composed
earlier, Pt. I in 1798, Pt. II in 1800. Scott had heard
een influenced by *Christabel* before he wrote the *Lay* in
it was known to Byron when he wrote *Mazeppa,* and
are other proofs that it had become accessible several

DATES

OF SOME OCCURRENCES IN MY OWN LIFE

A. D.

RICHARD HURD was born at Congreve, in the Parish of Penkrich, in the County of Stafford, January 13   1719-20

He was the second of three children, all sons, of John and Hannah Hurd; plain, honest, and good people; of whom he can truly say with the poet—

Si natura juberet, etc.

They rented a considerable farm at Congreve, when he was born; but soon after removed to a larger at Penford, about half way between Brewood and Wolverhampton in the same County.

There being a good Grammar School at Brewood, he was educated there under the Reverend Mr. Hillman, and, upon his death, under his successor, the Reverend Mr. Budworth—both well qualified for their office, and both very kind to him.

Mr. Budworth had been Master of the School at Rudgely; where he continued two years after his election to Brewood, while the School-house, which had been much neglected, was repairing. He was therefore sent to Rudgely immediately on Mr. Budworth's appointment to Brewood, returned with him to this place, and continued under his care, till he went to the University.

He must add one word more of his *second* Master. He knew him well, when he afterwards was of an age to judge of his merits. He had been a scholar of the famous Mr. Blackwell of Derby, and after-

wards bred at Christ's College in Cambridge, where
he resided till he had taken his M.A.'s degree. He
understood Greek and Latin well, and had a true
taste of the best writers in those languages. He
was, besides, a polite, well-bred man, and singularly attentive to the *manners*, in every sense of
the word, of his scholars. He had a warm sense
of virtue and religion, and enforced both with a
natural and taking eloquence. How happy, to
have had such a man, first, for his school-master,
and then for his friend.

Under so good direction, he was thought fit for
the University, and was accordingly admitted in
Emanuel College, in Cambridge, October 3,   .   1733
but did not go to reside there till a year or two
afterwards.

In this college, he was happy in receiving the
countenance, and in being permitted to attend the
Lectures, of that excellent Tutor, Mr. Henry Hub-
bard, although he had been admitted under
another person.

He took his B.A.'s degree in   .   .   .   1738–9
He took his M.A.'s degree, and was elected
fellow in   1742
Was ordained Deacon, 13th of June that year
in St. Paul's Cathedral, London, by Dr. Jos.
Butler, Bishop of Bristol and Dean of St. Paul's,
on Letters Dimissory from Dr. Gooch, Bishop of
Norwich.

Was ordained Priest, 20 May   .   .   .   1744
in the Chapel of Gonville and Caius College,
Cambridge, by the Bishop of Norwich, Dr. Gooch..
He took his B.D.'s degree in   1749

Poetica; which last book introduced him to the acquaintance of Mr. Warburton, by whose recommendation to the Bishop of London, Dr. Sherlock, he was appointed Whitehall Preacher in May

1749

1750

He published the Commentary on the Epistle to Augustus in . . . . . .

1751

— the new edition of both Comments, with Dedication to Mr. Warburton, in . . .

1753

— the Dissertation on the Delicacy of Friendship in . . . .

1755

His Father died November 27 this year, æt. 70.

He published the Remarks on Hume's Natural History of Religion in . . . . .

1757

Was instituted this year, Feb. 16, to the Rectory of Thurcaston, in the County of Leicester, on the presentation of Emanuel College.

He published Moral and Political Dialogues .

1759

He had the Sine-cure Rectory of Folkton, near Bridlington, Yorkshire, given him by the Lord Chancellor (Earl of Northington) on the recommendation of Mr. Allen, of Prior Park, near Bath, November 2, ...

1762

He published the Letters on Chivalry and Romance this year.

— Dialogues on Foreign Travel in

1763

And Letter to Dr. Leland of Dublin in

1764

He was made Preacher of Lincoln's Inn, on the recommendation of Mr. Charles Yorke, etc. November 6, ...

1765

Was collated to the Archdeaconry of Gloucester, on the death of Dr. Geekie, by the Bishop, August 27, ...

1767

Was appointed to open the Lecture of Bishop Warburton on Prophecy in . . . .

1768

He took the degree of D.D. at Cambridge Commencement this year.

A. D.

He published the Sermons on Prophecy in   1772

His Mother died February 27, 1773, æt. 88.   1773

He was consecrated Bishop of Lichfield and
Coventry, the 12th of February   1775

He published the 1st Volume of Sermons
preached at Lincoln's Inn   1776

And was made Preceptor to the Prince of Wales
and his brother Prince Frederick, the 5th of June
the same year.

Preached before the Lords, December 13, 1776,
first Fast for the War.

He lost his old and best friend, Bishop Warburton, June 7th .   .   .   .   .   .   [1779]

He published the 2nd and 3rd Volumes of Sermons in   .   .   .   .   [1780]

These three Volumes were published at the
desire of the Bench of Lincoln's Inn.

He was elected Member of the Royal Society of
Gottingen, January 11   1781

The Bishop of Winchester (Dr. Thomas) died
Tuesday, May 1, 1781. Received a gracious letter
from his Majesty the next morning, by a special
messenger from Windsor, with the offer of the See
of Worcester, in the room of Bishop North, to be
translated to Winchester, and of the Clerkship of
of the Closet, in the room of the late Bishop of
Winchester.

On his arrival at Hartlebury Castle in July that
year, resolved to put the Castle into complete
order, and to build a Library, which was much
wanted.

The Library was finished in   1782

and furnished with a collection of books, late
Bishop Warburton's, and ordered by his will to be

To these, other considerable additions have been since made.

Archbishop Cornwallis died in 1783.

Had the offer of the Archbishoprick from his Majesty, with many gracious expressions, and pressed to accept it; but humbly begged leave to decline it, as a charge not suited to his temper and talents, and much too heavy for him to sustain, especially in these times.

The King was pleased not to take offence at this freedom, and then to enter with him into some confidential conversation on the subject. It was offered to the Bishop of London, Dr. Lowth, and refused by him, as was foreseen, on account of his ill health. It was then given to Dr. Moore, Bishop of Bangor.

Added a considerable number of books to the new Library at Hartlebury in 1784

Confirmed Prince Edward (their Majesties' 4th son) in the Chapel of Windsor Castle, May 14th, 1785 1785

Added more books to the Library this year. 1785 And put the last hand (at least he thinks so) to the Bishop of Gloucester's Life, to be prefixed to the new edition of his works now in the press.

Confirmed Princess Augusta (their Majesties' second daughter) in the Chapel of Windsor Castle, December the 24th this year 1785

Preached in the Chapel the next day (Christmas Day) and administered the Sacrament to their Majesties and the Princess Royal and Princess Augusta.

Preached before their Majesties and Royal Family in the Chapel of Windsor Castle, and administered the Sacrament to them, on Christmas day 1786.

In the end of February this year .　.　.　was published in seven volumes 4to a complete 'edition of the works of Bishop Warburton. The *Life* is omitted for the present.

March 13, 1788, a fine gold Medal was this day given me by his Majesty at the Queen's House.

The King's head on one side. The Reverse was taken from a Seal of mine [a], which his Majesty chanced to see, and approved.

The Die was cut by Mr. Burch, and the Medal designed for the annual Prize-Dissertation on Theological Subjects in the University of Gottingen.

This summer the King came to Cheltenham to drink the waters, and was attended by the Queen, the Princess Royal, and the Princesses Augusta and Elizabeth. They arrived at Cheltenham in the evening of Saturday July the 12th, and resided in a house of Earl Falconberg. From Cheltenham they made excursions to several places in Gloucestershire and Worcestershire, and were every where received with joy by all ranks of people.

On Saturday, August the second, They were pleased to visit Hartlebury, at the distance of thirty-three miles, or more. The Duke of York came from London to Cheltenham the day defore, and was pleased to come with them. They arrived at Hartlebury at half an hour past eleven. Lord Courtoun, Mr. Digby (the Queen's Vice-Chamberlain), Col. Gwin (one of the King's Equerries), the

Countesses of Harcourt and Courtoun, composed
the suite. Their Majesties, after seeing the House,
breakfasted in the Library; and, when they had
reposed themselves some time, walked into the
Garden, and took several turns on the Terrases,
especially the Green Terras in the Chapel Garden.
Here they shewed themselves to an immense croud
of people, who flocked in from the neighbourhood,
and standing on the rising grounds in the Park,
saw, and were seen, to great advantage. The day
being extremely bright, the shew was agreeable
and striking. About two o'clock, their Majesties,
etc. returned to Cheltenham.

On the Tuesday following, August the fifth, Aug. 5
their Majesties, with the three Princesses, arrived
at 8 o'clock in the evening at the Bishop's Palace
in Worcester, to attend the charitable meeting of
the three Quires of Worcester, Hereford, and
Gloucester, for the benefit of the widows and
orphans of the poorer Clergy of those Dioceses;
which had been fixed, in consequence of the
signification of the King's intention to honour
that solemnity with his presence, for the 6th, 7th,
and 8th of that month.

The next morning a little before 10 o'clock, the
King was pleased to receive the compliments of
the Clergy. The Bishop, in the name of himself,
Dean and Chapter and Clergy of the Church and

---

b 'We, the Bishop and Dean and Chapter and Clergy of the
Church and Diocese of Worcester, humbly beg leave to present
our dutiful respects to your Majesty, and to express the joy we
feel on your Majesty's arrival at this place.
'Your presence, Sir, gladdens the hearts of your faithful
subjects, wherever you go. But We, the Clergy of this place, have
a peculiar cause to rejoice in the honour vouchsafed us at this
time; a time, devoted to an excellent charity for the relief of

Diocese, addressed the King in the Great Hall, in a short speech [b] to which his Majesty was pleased to return a gracious answer. He had then the honour to address the Queen in a few words, to which a gracious reply was made; and they had all the honour to kiss the King's and Queen's hand.

Soon after 10, the Corporation, by their Recorder, the Earl of Coventry, addressed and went through the same ceremony of kissing the King's hand. Then the King had a Levée in the Great Hall, which lasted till 11, when their Majesties, etc. walked through the Court of the Palace to the Cathedral, to attend divine Service and a Sermon. The Apparitor General, 2 Sextons, 2 Virgers, and 8 Beadsmen, walked before the King (as on great occasions they usually do before the Bishop); the Lord in waiting (Earl of Oxford) on the King's right hand, and the Bishop in his lawn on the left. After the King, came the Queen and Princesses,

---

a most deserving, though unfortunate part of our Order. This gracious notice and countenance of us at such a moment, shews, as your whole life has invariably done, your zealous concern for the interests of Religion, and the credit of its Ministers. And we trust, Sir, that we entertain a due sense of this goodness; and that we shall never be wanting in the most dutiful attachment to your Majesty's sacred person, to your august house, and to your mild and beneficent government.

'In our daily celebration of the sacred offices, committed to our charge, we make it our fervent prayer to Almighty God, that He will be pleased to take your Majesty into his special protection; and that your Majesty may live long, very long, in health and honour, to be the blessing and the delight of all your people.'

attended by the Countesses of Pembroke and Harcourt (Ladies of the Bed-chamber), and the Countess of Courtown, and the rest of their Suite. At the entrance of the Cathedral, their Majesties were received by the Dean and Chapter in their Surplices and hoods, and conducted to the foot of the stairs leading to their seat in a Gallery prepared and richly furnished by the Stewards [c] for their use, at the bottom of the Church near the West window.

The same ceremony was observed the two following days, on which they beared sacred musick, but without prayers or a sermon. On the last day August 8th, the King was pleased to give £200 to the charity: and in the evening attended a concert in the College Hall for the benefit of the Stewards.

On Saturday morning, August 9th, the King and Queen, etc. returned to Cheltenham.

Aug. 9

During their Majesties' stay at the Palace, they attended prayers in the Chapel of the Palace every morning (except the first, when the service was performed in the Church) which were read by the Bishop.

The King at parting was pleased to put into my hands for the poor of the City £50, and the Queen £50 more ; which I desired the Mayor (Mr. Davis) to see distributed amongst them in a proper manner.

The King also left £300 in my hands towards releasing the Debtors in the County and City Jails.

During the three days at Worcester, the concourse of people of all ranks was immense, and the

---

[c] Edward Foley, Esq., Member of Parliament for the County, and William Langford, D.D., late Prebendary of Worcester.

joy universal. The weather was uncommonly fine.
And no accident of any kind interrupted the
mutual satisfaction, which was given, and received,
on this occasion.

On Saturday, August 16, the King and Royal
Family left Cheltenham, and returned that evening to Windsor.

In the beginning of November following, the
King was seized with that illness, which was so
lamented. It continued till the end of February
1789, when his Majesty happily recovered.

Soon after I had his Majesty's command to
attend him at Kew; and on March 15, I administered the Sacrament to his Majesty at
Windsor in the Chapel of the Castle, as also on
Easter Sunday, April 12, and preached both days.

At the Sacrament of March 15, the King was
attended only by three or four of his Gentlemen :
On Easter-day, the Queen, Princess Royal, and
Princesses Augusta and Elizabeth, with several
Lords and Gentlemen and Ladies of the Court,
attended the King to the Chapel, and received the
Sacrament with him.

On April 23 (St. George's Day) a public thanks-
giving for the King's recovery was appointed. His
Majesty, the Queen, and Royal Family, with the
two Houses of Parliament, etc. went in procession
to St. Paul's. The Bishop of London preached.
I was not well enough to be there.

May 28, 1790, the Duke of Montagu died. He
was a nobleman of singular worth and virtue ; of
an exemplary life ; and of the best principles in
Church and State. As Governor to the Prince of
Wales and Prince Frederick, he was very attentive

propriety and dignity. The Preceptor was 1790
honoured with his confidence : and there never
was the least misunderstanding between them ;
or so much as a difference of opinion as to the
manner in which the education of the Princes
should be conducted.

In October 1790, I had the honour to receive
from the King the present of two fine full-length
pictures of his Majesty and the Queen, copied from
those at the Queen's House, St. James's Park,
painted by the late Mr. Gainsborough.

These pictures are put up in the great Drawing-
room at the Palace in Worcester, and betwixt
them, over the fire-place, is fixed an oval tablet
of white marble with the following Inscription in
Gold Letters.

' Hospes,

Imagines, quas contemplaris,

Augustorum Principum,

Georgii III, et Charlottæ Conjugis,

Rex ipse

Richardo Episcopo Vigorniensi

Donavit,

1790.'

My younger Brother, Mr. Thomas Hurd, of 1791
Birmingham, died on Saturday, September 17, Sept. 17
1791.

My elder Brother, Mr. John Hurd, of Hatton, 1792
near Shifnal, died on Thursday, December 6, Dec. 6
1792.

My noble and honoured friend, the Earl of 1793
Mansfield, died March 20, 1793. March 20

My old and much esteemed friend, Dr. Balguy, 1795
Prebendary and Archdeacon of Winchester, died Jan. 19
January 19, 1795.

A. D.

The Life of Bishop Warburton, which was sent
to the press in Autumn last, was not printed off
till the end of January, nor published till towards   1795
the end of February this year.   Feb. 24

Printed in the course of this year at the Kidderminster press a Collection of Bishop Warburton's
Letters to me, to be published after my death for
the benefit of the Worcester Infirmary.—The
edition consisted of 250 Copies, 4to—was finished
at the press in the beginning of December.   Dec. 1

In the Summer of 1796 visited my Diocese in   1796
person, I have great reason to suppose for the   June
last time; being in the 77th year of my age—*fiat*   17 to 30
voluntas Dei!

Mrs. Stafford Smith, late Mrs. Warburton, died
at Fladbury, September 1, 1796.   Sept. 1

Mr. Mason died at Aston, April 5, 1797. He   1797
was one of my oldest and most respected friends.   April 5th
How few of this description now remain!

By God's great mercy enter this day (24th   1799
January 1799) into my 80th year. Ps. xc. 10.   Jan. 24
But see, 1 Cor. xv. 22. Rom. viii. 18. 1 Pet. i. 3-5.
χάρις τῷ Θεῷ ἐπὶ τῇ ἀνεκδιηγήτῳ αὐτοῦ δωρεᾷ.
2 Cor. ix. 15.

It pleased God that I was able this Summer to   May 27 to
confirm over all parts of my Diocese.   June 14

And to visit my Diocese in person once more   1800
in June 1800.—L.D.   June 6 to 17

Lost my old and worthy friend Dr. Heberden,   1801
in the 91st or 92nd year of his age, May 16, 1801.   May 16

Consecrated, on Tuesday the 15th of June, 1802,   1802
the new Church and Churchyard of Lower Eating-   June 15

A.D.

Visited my Diocese by Commission—Commissioners, Dr. Arnold, my Chancellor, and Dr. Evans, Archdeacon.

1803
May 31 to
June 3

St. James' day, July 25, 1804, held an Ordination in Hartlebury Chapel—3 Deacons, 5 Priests—the last I can expect to undertake.

1804
July 25

Confirmations by the Bishop of Chester (Dr. Majendie). March 27, Stratford.

1805
March 27

    28, Bromsgrove.

28

    29, Hales Owen.

29

— by the Bishop of Hereford (Dr. Cornwall). June 14, Worcester.

June 14

 15, Pershore.

15

 17, Kidderminster

17

Visited my Diocese this year by Commission—Commissioners,

1806

The Chancellor and Archdeacon.

Warwick . . . . May 26.	
Worcester . . . . 28.	
Kidderminster . . 30.	
Pershore . . . . 31.	

1807, September 26. The Prince of Wales visited Lady Downshire, at Ombersley Court this month. I was too infirm to wait upon him either at Ombersley or Worcester ; but his Royal Highness was pleased to call at Hartlebury, on Saturday the 26th of this month, attended by his brother the Duke of Sussex, and Lord Lake, and staid with me above an hour.

1807

Sept. 26

1808, April 23. Granted a Commission to the Bishop of Chester, (Dr. Majendie), to consecrate the new Chapel and burying-ground at Red-Ditch, in the parish of Tardebig; which was performed this day, Thursday, April 21, 1808, the proper officers of the Court, and two of my Chaplains attending.

1808

"To this short narrative (the last paragraph of which was written by the author only five weeks before his death) little more will be added.

So late as the first Sunday in February before his death, though then declining in health and strength, he was able to attend his Parish Church, and to receive the Sacrament. Free from any painful or acute disorder, he gradually became weaker, but his faculties continued perfect. After a few days' confinement to his bed, he expired in his sleep on Saturday morning, May 28, 1808, having completed four months beyond his eighty-eighth year. He was buried in Hartlebury churchyard, according to his own directions.

He had been Bishop of Worcester for almost twenty-seven years; a longer period than any Bishop of that See since the Reformation."

DIALOGUE III.

ON THE

Golden Age of Queen *Elisabeth*:

BETWEEN

The Hon. ROBERT DIGBY, Dr. ARBUTHNOT,

and Mr. ADDISON.

OCCASIONED BY

A View of KENELWORTH CASTLE, in the Year 1716.

Hæc genera virtutum non solum in moribus nostris, sed vix jam in libris reperiuntur : Chartæ quoque, quæ illam pristinam severitatem continebant, obsoleverunt.

Cicero.

DIALOGUE III.

On the Age of Queen ELIZABETH.

MR. DIGBY, DR. ARBUTHNOT, MR. ADDISON.

IT happened, in the summer of the year 1716, that Dr. ARBUTHNOT and Mr. ADDISON had occasion to take a journey together into *Warwickshire*. Mr. DIGBY, who had received intelligence of their motions, and was then at *Coleshill*, contrived to give them the meeting at *Warwick*; where they intended to pass a day or two, in visiting the curiosities of that fine town, and the more remarkable of those remains of antiquity that are to be seen in its neighbourhood. These were matter of high entertainment to all of them; to Dr. ARBUTHNOT, for the pleasure of recollecting the ancient times; to Mr. ADDISON, on account of some political reflexions, he was fond of indulging on such occasions; and to Mr. DIGBY, from an ingenuous curiosity, and the love of seeing and observing whatever was most remarkable, whether in the past ages, or the present.

AMONGST other things that amused them, they were

it's many old monuments recalled to their memory [*f*]. The famous inscription of Sir FULK GREVIL occasioned some reflexions ; especially to Mr. DIGBY, who had used to be much affected with the fame and fortunes of the accomplished Sir PHILIP SIDNEY. The glory of the house of WARWICK was, also, an ample field of meditation. But what chanced to take their attention most, was the monument of the great earl of LEICESTER. It recorded his titles at full length, and was, besides, richly decorated with sculpture, displaying the various ensigns and trophies of his greatness. The pride of this minister had never appeared to them so conspicuous, as in the legends and ornaments of his tombstone ; which had not only outlived his family, but seemed to assure itself of immortality, by taking refuge, as it were, at the foot of the altar.

THESE funeral honours engaged them in some common reflexions on the folly of such expedients to perpetuate human grandeur ; but at the same time, as is the usual effect of these things, struck their imaginations very strongly. They readily apprehended what must have been the state of this mighty favourite in his lifetime, from what they saw of it in this proud memorial, which continued in a manner to insult posterity so many years after his death. But understanding that the fragments at least of his supreme glory, when it was flourishing at its height, were still

[*f*] For the account of these *Monuments*, and of *Kenelworth-Castle*, see the plans and descriptions of DUGDALE.

to

to be seen at KENELWORTH, which they knew could be at no great distance, they resolved to visit them the next day, and indulge to the utmost the several reflexions which such scenes are apt to inspire. On inquiry, they found it was not more than five or six miles to the castle; so that, by starting early in the morning, they might easily return to dinner at *Warwick*. They kept to their appointment so well, that they got to *Kenelworth* in good time, and had even two or three hours on their hands to spend, in taking an exact view of the place.

It was luckily one of those fine days, which our travellers would most have wished for, and which indeed are most agreeable in this season. It was clear enough to afford a distinct prospect of the country, and to set the objects, they wanted to take a view of, in a good light; and yet was so conveniently clouded as to check the heat of the sun, and make the exercise of walking, of which they were likely to have a good deal, perfectly easy to them.

WHEN they alighted from the coach, the first object that presented itself was the principal GATE-WAY of the Castle. It had been converted into a farm-house, and was indeed the only part of these vast ruins that was inhabited. On their entrance into the *inner-court*, they were struck with the sight of many mouldering towers, which preserved a sort of magnificence even in their ruins. They amused themselves with observing the vast compass of the whole, with marking the uses, and tracing the dimensions, of the several parts. All which it was easy for them to do, by the very distinct traces that remained of them, and especially by means of DUGDALE's plans and descriptions, which they had taken care to consult.

AFTER rambling about for some time, they clambered up a heap of ruins, which lay on the west side the court : and thence came to a broken tower, which, when they had mounted some steps, led them out into a path-way on the tops of the walls. From this eminence they had a very distinct view of the several parts they had before contemplated ; of the *gardens* on the north-side ; of the *winding meadow* that encompassed the walls of the castle, on the west and south ; and had, besides, the command of the country round about them for many miles. The prospect of so many antique towers falling into rubbish, contrasted to the various beauties of the landscape, struck them with admiration, and kept them silent for some time.

AT length recovering himself, I perceive, said Dr. ARBUTHNOT, we are all of us not a little affected with the sight of these ruins. They even create a melancholy in me ; and yet a melancholy of so delightful a kind, that I would not exchange it, me-thinks, for any brisker sensation. The experience of this effect hath often led me to inquire, how it is that

the

the mind, even while it laments, finds so great a pleasure in visiting these scenes of desolation. Is it, continued he, from the pure love of antiquity, and the amusing train of reflexions into which such remains of ancient magnificence naturally lead us?

I KNOW not, returned Mr. ADDISON, what pain it may give you to contemplate these triumphs of time and fortune. For my part, I am not sensible of the mixt sensation you speak of. I feel a pleasure indeed; but it is sincere, and, as I conceive, may be easily accounted for. 'Tis nothing more, I believe, than a fiction of the imagination, which makes me think I am taking a revenge on the once prosperous and overshadowing height, PRÆUMBRANS FASTIGIUM, as somebody expresses it, of inordinate Greatness. It is certain, continued he, this theatre of a great states-man's pride, the delight of many of our princes, and which boasts of having given entertainment to one of them in a manner so splendid, as to claim a remem-brance, even in the annals of our country, would now, in its present state, administer ample matter for much insulting reflection.

" WHERE, one might ask, are the tilts and tourna-ments, the princely shows and sports, which were once so proudly celebrated within these walls? Where are the pageants, the studied devices and emblems of curious invention, that set the court at a gaze, and

Where now, pursued he, (pointing to that which was formerly a canal, but at present is only a meadow with a small rivulet running through it) where is the floating island, the blaze of torches that eclipsed the day, the lady of the lake, the silken nymphs her attendants, with all the other fantastic exhibitions surpassing even the whimsies of the wildest romance ? What now is become of the revelry of feasting ? of the minstrelsy, that took the ear so delightfully as it babbled along the valley, or floated on the surface of this lake ? See there the smokeless kitchens, stretching to a length that might give room for the sacrifice of a hecatomb ; the vaulted hall, which mirth and jollity have set so often in an uproar ; the rooms of state, and the presence-chamber : what are they now but void and tenantless ruins, clasped with ivy, open to wind and weather, and representing to the eye nothing but the ribs and car-case, as it were, of their former state ? And see, said he, that proud gate-way, once the mansion of a surly porter [g], who, partaking of the pride of his lord, made

the

[g] The speaker's idea of Lord LEICESTER's porter agrees with the character he sustained on the queen's reception at *Kenelworth* ; as we find it described in a paper of good authority written at that time. " Here a PORTER, tall of person, big of limbs, stark of countenance—with club and keys of quantity according ; in a rough speech, full of passion in metre, while the queen came within his ward, burst out in a great pang of impatience to see such uncouth trudging to and fro, such riding in and out, with such din and noise of talk, within his charge ; whereof he never saw the like, nor had any warning once, ne yet could make to himself any cause of the matter. At last, upon better view and advertisement, he proclaims open gates and free passage to all ;

yields

the crowds wait, and refused admittance, perhaps, to nobles whom fear or interest drew to these walls, to pay their homage to their master : see it now the residence of a poor tenant, who turns the key but to let himself out to his daily labour, to admit him to a short meal, and secure his nightly slumbers. Yet, in this humble state, it hath had the fortune to outlive the glory of the rest, and hath even drawn to itself the whole of that little note and credit which time hath continued to this once pompous building. For, while the castle itself is crumbled into shapeless ruins, and is prophaned, as we there see, by the vilest uses, this outwork of greatness is left entire, sheltered and closed in from bird and beast, and even affords some decent room in which the *human face divine* is not ashamed to shew itself."

WHILE Mr. ADDISON went on in this vein, his two friends stood looking on each other ; as not conceiving what might be the cause of his expressing himself with a vehemence, so uncommon, and not suited to his natural temper. When the fit was over, I confess, said Dr. ARBUTHNOT, this is no bad topic for a moralist to declaim upon. And, though it be a trite one, we know how capable it is of being adorned by him who, on

yields over his club, his keys, his office and all, and on his knees humbly prays pardon of his ignorance and impatience. Which her highness graciously granting, &c."—
A letter from an attendant in court to his friend a citizen and

a late occasion, could meditate so finely on the Tombs at Westminster [b]. But surely, proceeded he, you warm yourself in this contemplation, beyond what the subject requires of you. The vanity of human greatness is seen in so many instances, that I wonder to hear you harangue on this with so peculiar an exultation. There is no travelling ten miles together in any part of the kingdom without stumbling on some ruin, which, though perhaps not so considerable as this before us, would furnish occasion, however, for the same reflexions. There would be no end of moralizing over every broken tower, or shattered fabric, which calls to mind the short-lived glories of our ancestors.

True, said Mr. Addison ; and, if the short continuance of these glories were the only circumstance, I might well have spared the exultation, you speak of, in this triumph over the shattered remnants of *Kenelworth*. But there is something else that fires me on the occasion. It brings to mind the fraud, the rapine, the insolence, of the potent minister, who vainly thought to immortalize his ill-gotten glory by this proud monument. Nay, further, it awakens an indignation against the prosperous tyranny of those wretched times, and creates a generous pleasure in reflecting on the happiness we enjoy under a juster and more equal government. Believe me, I never see the remains of that greatness which arose in the past ages on the ruins of public freedom and private property, but I con-

[b] In the first volume of the Spectator.

gratulate

gratulate with myself on living at a time, when the meanest subject is as free and independent as those royal minions ; and when his property, whatever it be, is as secure from oppression, as that of the first minister. And I own this congratulation is not the less sincere for considering that the instance before us is taken from the reign of the virgin queen, which it hath been the fashion to cry up above that of any other of our princes [i].   I desire no other confutation of so strange unthankful a preference, than the sight of this vast castle, together with the recollection of those means by which its master arrived at his enormous greatness.

YOUR indignation then, replied Dr. ARBUTHNOT, is not so much of the moral, as *political* kind [k].   But is not the conclusion a little too hasty, when, from the instance of one over-grown favourite, you infer the general infelicity of the time, in which he flourished ? I am not, I assure you, one of those unthankful men who forget the blessings they enjoy under a prince of more justice and moderation than queen ELIZABETH, and under a better constitution of government than

[i] The factious use, that was afterwards made of this humour of magnifying the character of ELIZABETH, may be seen in the *Craftsman* and *Remarks on the History of England*.

[k] What the *political* character of Mr. ADDISON was, may be seen from his *Whig-examiner*. This amiable man was keen and even caustic on subjects, where his party, that is, *civil liberty*, was concerned. Nor let it be any objection to the character I make him sustain in this Dialogue, that he treats ELIZABETH'S govern-

prevailed in the days of our forefathers. Yet, setting aside some particular dishonours of that reign (of which, let the tyranny of *Leicester*, if you will, be one), I see not but the acknowledged virtues of that princess, and the wisdom of her government, may be a proper foundation for all the honours that posterity have ever paid to her.

WERE I even disposed to agree with you, returned Mr. ADDISON, I should not have the less reason for triumphing, as I do, on the present state of our government. For, if such abuses could creep in, and be suffered for so many years under so great a princess, what was there not to fear (as what, indeed, did not the subject actually feel) under some of her successors? But, to speak my mind frankly, I see no sufficient grounds for the excessive prejudice, that hath somehow taken place, in favour of the GOLDEN REIGN, as it is called, OF ELIZABETH. I find neither the wisdom, nor the virtue in it, that can entitle it to a preference before all other ages.

ON the contrary, said Dr. ARBUTHNOT, I never contemplate the monuments of that time, without a silent admiration of the virtues that adorned it. Heroes and sages crowd in upon my memory. Nay, the very people were of a character above what we are acquainted with in our days. I could almost fancy, the soil itself wore another face, and, as you poets imagine on some occasions, that our ancestors lived under a brighter sun and happier climate than we can boast of.

To

To be sure! said Mr. ADDISON smiling: or, why not affirm, in the proper language of romance, that the women of those days were all chaste, and the men valiant? But cannot you suspect at least that there is some enchantment in the case, and that your love of antiquity may possibly operate in more instances than those of your favourite *Greeks* and *Romans?* Tell me honestly, pursued he, hath not this distance of a century and half a little imposed upon you? Do not these broken towers, which moved you just now to so compassionate a lamentation over them, dispose you to a greater fondness for the times in which they arose, than can be fairly justified?

I WILL not deny, returned Dr. ARBUTHNOT, but we are often very generous to the past times, and unjust enough to the present. But I think there is little of this illusion in the case before us. And, since you call my attention to these noble ruins, let me own to you, that they do indeed excite in me a veneration for the times of which they present so striking a memorial. But surely not without reason. For there is scarce an object in view, that doth not revive the memory of some distinguishing character of that age, which may justify such veneration.

ALAS! interrupted Mr. ADDISON, and what can these objects call to mind but the memory of barbarous

FOR the *government*, replied Dr. ARBUTHNOT, I do not well conceive how any conclusion about that can be drawn from this fabric. The MANNERS I was thinking of; and I see them strongly expressed in many parts of it. But whether barbarous or not, I could almost take upon me to dispute with you. And why, indeed, since you allowed yourself to declaim on the vices, so apparent, as you suppose, in this monument of antiquity, may not I have leave to consider it in another point of view, and present to you the virtues which, to my eye at least, are full as discernible?

YOU cannot, continued he, turn your eyes on any part of these ruins, without encountering some memorial of the virtue, industry, or ingenuity, of our ancestors.

LOOK there, said he, on that fine room (pointing to the HALL, that lay just beneath them); and tell me if you can help respecting the HOSPITALITY which so much distinguished the palaces of the great in those simpler ages. You gave an invidious turn to this circumstance, when you chose to consider it only in the light of wasteful expence and prodigality. But no virtue is privileged from an ill name. And, on second thoughts, I persuade myself, it will appear you have injured this, by so uncandid an appellation. Can it deserve this censure, that the lord of this princely castle threw open his doors and spread his table for the

reception

reception of his friends, his followers, and even for the royal entertainment of his sovereign ? Is any expence more proper than that which tends to concilitate [*l*] friendships, spread the interests of society, and knit mankind together by a generous communication in these advantages of wealth and fortune ? The arts of a refined sequestered luxury were then unknown. The same bell, that called the great man to his table, invited the neighbourhood all around, and proclaimed a holiday to the whole country [*m*]. Who does not feel the decorum, and understand the benefits of this magnificence ? The pre-eminence of rank and fortune was nobly sustained : the subordination of society preserved : and yet the envy, that is so apt to attend the great, happily avoided. Hence the weight and influence of the old nobility, who engaged the love, as well as commanded the veneration, of the people. In the mean time, rural industry flourished : private luxury

[*l*] LUCIAN expresses this use of the Table, prettily—ΦΙΛΙΑΣ ΜΕΣΙΤΗΝ ΤΡΑΠΕΖΑΝ, Ἐρωτες c. 27.

[*m*] Besides this sort of hospitality, there was another still more noble and disinterested, which distinguished the early times, especially the purer ages of chivalry. It was customary, it seems, for the great lords to fix up HELMETS on the roofs and battlements of their castles as a signal of hospitality to all adventurers and noble passengers. " Adoncques etoit une coustume en la Grant Bretagne (says the author of the old romance, called PERCE-FOREST) et fut tant que charité regna illecque, tous gentils hommes et nobles dames faisoient mettre au plus hault de leur hostel ung heaulme, en SIGNE que tous gentils hommes et gentilles femmes trespassans les chemins, entrassent hardyement en leur hostel

was discouraged: and in both ways that frugal simplicity of life, our country's grace and ornament in those days, was preserved and promoted.

It would spoil your panegyric, I doubt, said Mr. Addison, to observe the factious use, that was made of this magnificence, and the tendency it had to support the pride and insolence of the old nobility. The interest of the great, I am afraid, was but another name for the slavery of the people [n].

I see it, Dr. Arbuthnot said, in a different light; and so did our princes themselves, who could not but be well acquainted with the proper effects of that interest. They considered the weight of the nobility, as a counterpoise to their own sovereignty. It was on this account they had used all means to lessen their influence. But the consequence was beside their expectation. The authority of the crown fell with it: and, which was still less expected by political men, the liberty of the people, after it had wantoned for a time, sunk

[n] This is not said without authority: "Give me leave, says "one, to hold this paradox, that the English were never more "idle, never more ignorant in manual arts, never more factious "in following the parties of princes or their landlords, never "more base (as I may say) trencher slaves, than in that age, "wherein great men kept open houses for all comers and goers: "and that in our age, wherein we have better learned each man "to live of his own, and great men keep not such troops of idle "servants, not only the English are become very industrious "and skilful in manual arts, but also the tyranny of lords and "gentlemen is abated, whereby they nourished private dissen- "sions and civil wars, with the destruction of the common "people." Fynes Moryson's *Itinerary*, Part III. Ch. v.

under

under the general oppression. It was then discovered, but a little of the latest, that public freedom throve best, when it wound itself about the stock of the ancient nobility. In truth, it was the defect, not the excess, of patrician influence, that made way for the miseries of the next century.

You see then it is not without cause that I lay a stress, even in a political view, on this popular hospitality of the great in the former ages [o].

But, lest you think I sit too long at the table, let us go on to the TILTYARD, which lies just before us; that school of fortitude and honour to our generous forefathers. A younger fancy, than mine, would be apt to kindle at the sight. And our sprightlier friend here, I dare say, has already taken fire at the remembrance of the gallant exercises, which were celebrated in that quarter.

Mr. DIGBY owned, he had a secret veneration for the manly games of that time, which he had seen so triumphantly set forth in the old poets and romancers.

[o] Dr. ARBUTHNOT, too, has his authority. A famous politician of the last century expresseth himself to much the same purpose, after his manner: "Henceforth, says he, [that is, after the statutes against retainers in HEN. VII's reign] the country lives, and *great tables* of the nobility, which no longer nourished veins that would bleed for them, were fruitless and loathsome till they changed the air, and of princes became *courtiers*; where their revenues, never to have been exhausted by beef and mutton, were found *narrow*; whence followed racking of rents, and, at length, sale of lands." SIR JAMES HARRINGTON'S OCEANA, p. 40. *Lond.* 1656.

RIGHT, said Mr. ADDISON; it is precisely in that circumstance that the enchantment consists. Some of our best wits have taken a deal of idle pains to ennoble a very barbarous entertainment, and recommend it to us under the specious name of gallantry and honour. But Mr. DIGBY sees through the cheat. Not that I doubt, continued he, but the doctor, now he is in the vein of panegyric, will lay a mighty stress on these barbar[t]ities; and perhaps compare them with the exercises in the *Roman* Circus, or the *Olympic* Barriers.

AND why not? interrupted Dr. ARBUTHNOT. The tendency of all three was the same; to invigorate the faculties both of mind and body; to give strength, grace, and dexterity, to the limbs; and fire the mind with a generous emulation of the manly and martial virtues.

WHY truly, said Mr. ADDISON, I shall not deny that all *three*, as you observe, were much of the same merit. And, now your hand is in for this sort of encomium, do not forget to celebrate the sublime taste of our forefathers for *bear-baiting* [*p*], as well as *tilting*; and tell

us

[*p*] True it is, that this divertisement of *bear-baiting* was not altogether unknown in the age of ELIZABETH, and, as it seemeth, not much misliked of master STOW himself, who hath very graphically described-it. He is speaking of the *Danish* embassador's reception and entertainment at *Greenwich* in 1586.
"As

us too, how gloriously the mob of those days, as well as their betters, used to belabour one another.

I CONFESS, said Dr. ARBUTHNOT, the softness of our manners makes it difficult to speak on this subject without incurring the ridicule, you appear so willing to employ against me. But you must not think to discredit these gymnastics by a little raillery, which has its foundation only in modern prejudices. For it is no secret that the gravest and politest men of antiquity were of my mind. You will hardly suspect PLATO of incivility, either in his notions or manners. And need I remind you how much he insists on the gymnastic discipline ; without which he could not have formed, or at least have supported, his republic ?

" As the better sort, saith he, had their convenient disports, so were not the ordinary people excluded from competent pleasure. For, upon a green, very spacious and large, where thousands might stand and behold with good contentment, their BEAR-BAITING and bull-baiting (tempered with other merry disports) were exhibited ; whereat it cannot be spoken of what pleasure the people took.

For it was a sport alone, of these beasts, continueth the historian, to see the bear with his pink-eyes leering after his enemies ; the nimbleness and wait of the dog to take his advantage ; and the force and experience of the bear again to avoid the assaults ; if he were bitten in one place, how he would pinch in another to get free ; and if he were once taken, then what shift with biting, clawing, roaring, tugging, grasping, tumbling, and tossing, he would work to wind himself away ; and, when he was loose, to shake his ears with the blood and slaver about his phisnomy, was a pittance of good relief. The like pastime also of the bull.—And now the day being far spent, and the sun in his declination, the embassador withdrew to his lodging by barge to CROSBY's place ; where, no doubt, THIS DAY'S SOLEMNITY

IT was upon this principle, I suppose then, said Mr. DIGBY, or perhaps in imitation of his *Grӕcian* master, that our MILTON laid so great a stress on this discipline in his TRACTATE OF EDUCATION. And before him, in the very time you speak of, ASCHAM, I observe, took no small pains to much the same purpose in his TOXOPHILUS.

IT is very clear, resumed Dr. ARBUTHNOT, from these instances, and many more that might be given, that the ancients were not singular in their notions on this subject. But, since you have drawn me into a grave defence of these exercises, let me further own to you that I think the *Gothic* Tilts and Tournaments exceeded, both in use and elegance, even the *Grӕcian* gymnastics [q]. They were a more direct image of war, than any of the games at *Olympia*. And if *Xenophon* could be so lavish in his praises on the *Persian* practice of hunting, because it had some resemblance to the exercise of arms, what would he not have said of an institution, which has all the forms of a real combat ?

BUT there was an elegance, too, in the conduct of the tournament, that might reconcile it even to modern delicacy. For, besides the splendor of the shew; the dexterity, with which these exercises were performed; and the fancy, that appeared in their accoutrement, dresses, and devices; the whole contest was ennobled

[q] See the *Anacharsis* of LUCIAN.

with

with an air of gallantry, that must have had a great effect in refining the manners of the combatants. And yet this gallantry had no ill influence on morals; for, as you insulted me just now, it was the odd humour of those days for the women to pride themselves in their chastity [r], as well as the men in their valour.

In short, I consider the *Tournay*, as the best school of civility as well as heroism "High-erected thoughts, seated in a heart of courtesy," as an old writer [s] well expresses it, was the proper character of such as had been trained in this discipline.

No wonder then, pursued he, the poets and romance-writers took so much pains to immortalize these trials of manhood. It was but what PINDAR and HOMER him-

[r] If the reader be complaisant enough to admit the fact, it may be accounted for, on the ideas of chivalry, in the following manner. The knight forfeited all pretensions to the favour of the ladies, if he failed, in any degree, in the point of valour. And, reciprocally, the claim which the ladies had to protection and courtesy from the order of knights, was founded singly in the reputation of chastity, which was the female point of honour. "Ce droit que les dames avoient sur la chevalerie (says M. DE LA CURNE DE STE PALAVE) devoit étre conditionel; il supposoit que leur conduite et leur reputation ne les rendoient point indignes de l'espece d'association qui les unissoit à cet ordre uniquement fondé sur l'honneur.

self, those ancient masters of romance, had done before them. And how could it be otherwise ? The shew itself, as I said, had something very taking in it ; whilst every graceful attitude of person, with every generous movement of the mind, afforded the finest materials for description. And I am even ready to believe, that what we hear censured in their writings, as false, incredible, and fantastic, was frequently but a just copy of life, and that there was more of truth and reality [t] in their representations, than we are apt to imagine. Their notions of honour and gallantry were carried to an elevation [u], which, in these degenerate days,

[t] What is hinted, here, of the *reality* of these representations, hath been lately shewn at large in a learned memoir on this suj⟨b⟩ect, which the reader will find in the xx[th] Tom. of HIST. DE L'ACAD. DES INSCRIPTIONS ET BELLES LETTRES.

[u] This represen⟨ta⟩tion of things in the ages of chivalry agrees with what we are told by the author of the memoir just quoted : " Les premières leçons," [says he, speaking of the manner in which the youth were educated in the houses of the Great, which were properly the schools of those times] " qu'on leur donnoit, regardoient principalement *l'amour de Dieu, et des dames*, e'est-à-dire, la religion, et la galanterie. Mais autant la dévotion qu'on leur inspiroit étoit accompagnée de puerilités et de superstitions, autant l'amour des dames, qu'on leur recommandoit, étoit il rempli de RAFFINEMENT et de FANATISME. Il semble qu'on ne pouvoit, dans ces siécles ignorans et grossiers, présenter aux hommes la religion sous une forme assez materielle pour la mettre à leur portée ;   ni leur donner, en même tems, une idée de l'amour assez pure, assez metaphysique, pour prevenir les desordres et les excès, dont etoit capable une nation qui conservoit par-tout le caractere impetueux qu'elle montroit à la guerre." Tom. xx. p. 600.

One sees then the origin of that furious gallantry which runs through the old romances. And so long as the *refinement and fanaticism*, which the writer speaks of, were kept in full vigour
by

days, hurts the credit of their story ; just as I have met with men that have doubted whether the virtues of the REGULI and the SCIPIOS of ancient fame were not the offspring of pure fancy.

NAY now, Dr. ARBUTHNOT, said Mr. ADDISON, you grow quite extravagant. What you, who are used to be so quick at espying all abuses in science, and defects in good taste, turn advocate for these fopperies !

by the force of institution and the fashion of the times, the morals of these enamoured knights might, for any thing I know, be as pure as their apologist represents them. At the same time it must be confessed that this discipline was of a nature very likely to relax itself under another state of things, and certainly to be misconstrued by those who should come to look upon these pictures of a *refined and spiritual passion*, as incredible and fantastic. And hence, no doubt, we are to account for that censure which a famous writer, and one of the ornaments of ELIZABETH's own age, passeth on the old books of chivalry. His expression is downright, and somewhat coarse. " In our fathers time nothing was read but books of chivalry, wherein a man by reading should be led to none other end, but only to *manslaughter* and *baudrye*. If any man suppose they were good enough to pass the time withall, he is deceived. For surely vain words do work no small thing in vain, ignorant, and young minds, especially if they be given any thing thereunto of their own nature." He adds, like a good Protestant, " These books, as I have heard say, were made the most part in abbayes and monasteries; a very likely and fit fruit of such an idle and blind kind of living." *Præf. to* ASCHAM'S TOXOPHILUS, 1571.
I thought it but just to set down this censure of Mr. ASCHAM over-against the candid representation of the French memorialist. —However, what is said of the influence, which this ancient institution had on the character of his countrymen, is not to be disputed. " Les preceptes d'amour repandoient dans le commerce des dames ces considerations et ces egards respectueuxt qui, n'ayant jamais été effacés de l'esprit des François, on, toujours fait un des caractères distinctifs de nôtre nation."

Mr.

Mr. DIGBY and I shall begin to think you banter us, in this apology for the ancient gymnastics, and are only preparing a chapter for the facetious memoirs [w], you sometimes promise us.

NEVER more in earnest, I assure you, replied the doctor. I know what you have to object to these pictures of life and manners. But, if they will not bear examining as copies, they may deserve to be imitated as models. And their use, methinks, might atone for some defects in the article of probability.

FOR my part, I consider the legends of ancient chivalry in a very serious light,

> As *niches*, fill'd with statues to invite
> Young valours forth—[x]

as BEN JONSON, a valorous hardy poet, and who, himself, would have made a good knight-errant, justly says of them. For, it is certain, they had this effect. The youth, in general, were fired with the love of martial exercises. They were early formed to habits of fatigue and enterprise. And, together with this warlike spirit, the profession of chivalry was favourable to every other virtue. Affability, courtesy, generosity, veracity, these were the qualifications most pretended to by the men of arms, in the days of pure and uncorrupted chivalry. We do not perhaps, ourselves, know, at this distance of

[w] Of SCRIBLERUS. See the vi[th] chapter of that learned work *On the ancient Gymnastics.*
[x] MASQUES, p. 181. WHALEY's edition.

time,

time, how much we are indebted to the force of this singular institution. But this I may presume to say, that the men, among whom it arose and flourished most, had prodigious obligations to it. No policy, even of an ancient legislator, could have contrived a better expedient to cultivate the manners and tame the spirits of a rude and ignorant people. I could almost fancy it providentially introduced among the northern na-tions, to break the fierceness of their natures, and prevent that brutal savageness and ferocity of character, which must otherwise have grown upon them in the darker ages.

NAY, the generous sentiments, it inspired, perhaps contributed very much to awaken an emulation of a different kind ; and to bring on those days of light and knowledge which have disposed us, somewhat unthankfully, to vilify and defame it. This is certain, that the first essays of wit and poetry, those harbingers of returning day to every species of good letters, were made in the bosom of chivalry, and amidst the assem-blies of noble dames, and courteous knights. And we may even observe, that the best of our modern princes, such as have been most admired for their personal virtues, and have been most concerned in restoring all the arts of civility and politeness, have been passionately addicted to the feats of ancient prowess. In the num-ber of these, need I remind you of the courts of FRANCIS I, and HENRY IV, to say nothing of our own

virtues in one, our renowned and almost romantic
ELIZABETH [y] ?

[y] This romantic spirit of the Queen may be seen as well in
her *amours*, as military atchievements. "Ambiri, coli ob for-
mam, et AMORIBUS, etiam inclinatâ jam ætate, videri voluit;
de FABULOSIS INSULIS per illam relaxationem renovatâ quasi
memoriâ in quibus EQUITES AC STRENUI HOMINES ERRABANT, et
AMORES, foeditate omni prohibitâ, generosè per VIRTUTEM exerce-
bant." THUANI Hist. tom. vi. p. 172.

The observation of the great historian is confirmed by FRANCIS
OSBORNE, Esq. who, speaking of a contrivance of the *Cecilian*
party to ruin the earl of ESSEX, by giving him a rival in the good
graces of the queen, observes—" But the whole result concluding
in a duel, did rather inflame than abate the former account she
made of him : the opinion of a CHAMPION being more splendid
(in the weak and romantic sense of women, that admit of nothing
fit to be made the object of a quarrel but themselves) and far
above that of a captain or general. So as Sir EDMUND CARY,
brother to the Lord HUNSDON, then chamberlain and near
kinsman to the Queen, told me, that though she chid them
both, nothing pleased her better than a conceit she had that
her *beauty* was the subject of this quarrel, when, God knows,
it grew from the stock of honour, of which then they were very
tender."—MEM. OF Q. ELIZABETH, p. 456.

But nothing shews the romantic disposition of the Queen,
and indeed of her times, more evidently than the TRIUMPH, as
it was called; devised and performed with great solemnity,
in honour of the *French* commissioners in 1581. The contrivance
was for four of her principal courtiers, under the quaint appellation of " four foster-chidren of DESIRE," to besiege and carry,
by dint of arms, " THE FORTRESS OF BEAUTY ; " intending, by
this courtly ænigma, nothing less than the queen's majesty's
own person.—The actors in this famous triumph were, the Earl
of ARUNDEL, the Lord WINDSOR, Master PHILIP SIDNEY, and
Master FULK GREVIL." And the whole was conducted so entirely
in the spirit and language of knight errantry, that nothing in
the Arcadia itself is more romantic. See the account at large
in STOW's continuation of HOLINSHED's Chronicles, p. 1316—1321.

To see the drift and propriety of this triumph, it is to be
observed that the business which brought the *French* commissioners
into *England* was, the great affair of the queen's marriage with the
duke of ALANÇON.

BUT

BUT you think I push the argument too far. And less than this may dispose you to conceive with reverence of the scene before us, which must ever be regarded as a nursery of brave men, a very seed-plot of warriors and heroes. I consider the successes at the barriers as preludes to future conquests in the field. And, as whimsical a figure as a young tilter may make in your eye, who will say that the virtue was not formed here, that triumphed at AXELL, and bled at ZUTPHEN ?

WE shall very readily, replied Mr. ADDISON, acknowledge the bravery and other virtues of the young hero, whose fortunes you hint at. He was, in truth, to speak the language of that time, the very flower of knighthood, and contributed more than any body else, by his pen, as well as sword, to throw a lustre on the profession of chivalry. But the thing itself, however adorned by his wit and recommended by his manners, was barbarous ; the offspring of *Gothic* fierceness ; and shews the times, which favoured it so much, to have scarcely emerged from their original rudeness and brutality. You may celebrate, as loudly as you please, the deeds of these wonder-working knights. Alas, what affinity have such prodigies to our life and manners ? The old poet, you quoted just now with approbation, shall tell us the difference :

These were bold stories of our *Arthur's* age:
But here are other acts, another stage

And

And scene appears; it is not since as then;
No giants, dwarfs, or monsters here, but MEN [z].

OR, if you want a higher authority, we should not, methinks, on such an occasion, forget the admirable CERVANTES, whose ridicule hath brought eternal dishonour on the profession of knight-errantry.

WITH your leave, interrupted Dr. ARBUTHNOT, I have reason to except against both your authorities. At best, they do but condemn the *abuses* of chivalry, and the madness of continuing the old romantic spirit in times when, from a change of manners and policy, it was no longer in season. Adventures, we will say, were of course to cease, when giants and monsters disappeared. And yet have they totally disappeared, and have giants and monsters been no where heard of out of the castles and forests of our old romancers? 'Tis odds, methinks, but, in the sense of ELIZABETH's good subjects, PHILIP II might be a *giant* at least; and, without a little of this adventurous spirit, it may be a question whether all her enchanters, I mean her BURLEIGHS and WALSINGHAMS, would have proved a match for him. I mention this the rather to shew you, how little obligation his countrymen have to your CERVANTES for laughing away the remains of that prowess, which was the best support of the *Spanish* monarchy.

[z] Speeches at Prince HENRY's barriers.

As

As if, said Mr. ADDISON, the prowess of any people were only to be kept alive by their running mad. But let the case of the *Spaniards* be what it will, surely we, of this country, have little obligation to the spirit of chivalry, if it were only that it produced, or encouraged at least, and hath now entailed upon us, the curse of duelling ; which even yet domineers in the fashionable world, in spite of all that wit, and reason, and religion itself, have done to subdue it. 'Tis true, at present this law of arms is appealed to only in the case of some high point of nice and mysterious honour. But in the happier days you celebrate, it was called in aid, on common occasions. Even questions of right and property, you know, were determined at[1] the barriers [a]: and brute force was allowed the most equitable, as well as shortest, way of deciding all disputes both concerning a man's estate and honour.

You might observe too, interposed Dr. ARBUTHNOT, that this was the way in which those fiercer disputes concerning a mistress, or a kingdom, were frequently decided. And, if this sort of decision, in such cases, were still in use among Christian princes, you might

[1 ar 1788].
[a] There was an instance of this kind, and perhaps the latest upon record in our history, in the 13th year of the queen, when "a combat was appointed to have been fought for a certain manor, and demain lands belonging thereto, in *Kent*." The matter was compromised in the end. But not till after the usual forms had been observed, by the two parties: of which we have a curious and circumstantial detail in *Holinshed's*

call it perhaps a barbarous custom : but would it be ever the worse, do you think, for their good subjects ?

PERHAPS it would not, returned Mr. ADDISON, in some instances. And yet will you affirm, that those *good subjects* were in any enviable situation, under their fighting masters ? After all, allowing you to put the best construction you can on these usages of our fore-fathers,
> " all we find
> Is, that they did their work and din'd."

And though such feats may argue a sound athletic constitution, you must excuse me, if I am not forward to entertain any high notions of their civility.

THEIR civility, said Dr. ARBUTHNOT, is another consideration. The HALL and TILT-YARD are certainly good proofs of what they are alleged for, the hospitality and bravery of our ancestors. But it hath not been maintained, that these were their only virtues. On the contrary, it seems to me, that every flower of humanity, every elegance of art and genius, was cultivated amongst them. For an instance, need we look any further than the LAKE, which in the flourishing times of this castle was so famous, and which we even now trace in the winding-bed of that fine meadow ?

I DO not understand you, replied Mr. ADDISON. I can easily imagine what an embellishment that lake must have been to the castle ; but am at a loss to con-

ceive

ceive what flowers of wit and ingenuity, to use your own ænigmatical language, could be raised or so much as watered by it.

AND have you then, returned Dr. ARBUTHNOT, so soon forgotten the large description, you gave us just now, of the shows and pageants displayed on this lake? And can any thing better declare the art, invention, and ingenuity, of their conductors? Is not this canal as good a memorial of the ardour and success with which the finer exercises of the mind were pursued in that time, as the tilt-yard, we have now left, is of the address and dexterity shewn in those of the body?

I REMEMBER, said Mr. ADDISON, that many of the shows, intended for the queen's entertainment at this place, were exhibited on that canal. But as to any art or beauty of contrivance—

"You see none, I suppose."

WHY truly none, resumed Mr. ADDISON. To me they seemed but well enough suited to the other barbarities of the time. "The Lady of the Lake and her train of Nereids," was not that the principal? And can it pass for any thing better than a jumble of *Gothic* romance and pagan fable? a barbarous modern conceit, varnished over with a little classical pedantry?

AND is that the best word you can afford, said Dr. ARBUTHNOT, to these ingenious devices? The business was, to welcome the Queen to this palace, and at the same time to celebrate the honours of her government. And what more decent way of complimenting a great Prince, than through the veil of fiction? Or what so elegant way of entertaining a learned Prince, as by working up that fiction out of the old poetical story? And if something of the *Gothic* romance adhered to these classical fictions, it was not for any barbarous pleasure, that was taken in this patchwork, but that the artist found means to incorporate them with the highest grace and ingenuity. For what, in other words, was the *Lady of the Lake* (the particular that gives most offence to your delicacy), but the presiding nymph of the stream, on which these shews were presented? And, if the contrivance was to give us this nymph under a name that romance had made familiar, what was this but taking advantage of a popular prejudice to introduce his fiction with more address and probability?

But see the propriety of the scene itself, for the designer's purpose, and the exact decorum with which these fanciful personages were brought in upon it. It was not enough, that the pagan deities were summoned to pay their homage to the queen. They were the deities of the fount and ocean, the watery nymphs and demi-gods: and these were to play their part in their own element. Could any preparation be more artful for the panegyric designed on the naval glory of that reign? Or, could any representation be more grateful

to

to the queen of the ocean, as ELIZABETH was then called, than such as expressed her sovereignty in those regions? Hence the sea-green Nereids, the Tritons, and Neptune himself, were the proper actors in the drama. And the opportunity of this spacious lake gave the easiest intro-duction and most natural appearance to the whole scenery. Let me add, too, in further commendation of the taste which was shewn in these agreeable fancies, that the attributes and dresses of the deities themselves were studied with care ; and the most learned poets of the time employed to make them speak and act in character. So that an old *Greek* or *Roman* might have applauded the contrivance, and have almost fancied himself assisting at a religious ceremony in his own country.

AND, to shew you that all this propriety was intended by the designer himself, and not imagined at pleasure by his encomiast ; I remember, that when, some years after, the earl of HERTFORD had the honour to receive the queen at his seat in *Hampshire*, because he had no such canal as this in readiness on the occasion, he set on a vast number of hands to hollow a bason in his park for that purpose. With so great diligence and so exact a decorum were these entertainments conducted !

DID not I tell you, interposed Mr. ADDISON, address-ing himself to Mr. DIGBY, to what an extravagance the doctor's admiration of the ancient times would

on the art, elegance, and decorum of THE PRINCELY PLEASURES OF KENELWORTH [b]? And must not it divert you to see the unformed genius of that age tricked out in the graces of *Roman* or even *Attic* politeness?

MR. DIGBY acknowledged, it was very generous in the doctor to represent in so fair a light the amusements of the ruder ages. But I was thinking, said he, to what cause it could possibly be owing, that these pagan fancies had acquired so general a consideration in the days of ELIZABETH.

THE general passion for these fancies, returned Dr. ARBUTHNOT, was a natural consequence of the revival of learning. The first books, that came into vogue, were the poets. And nothing could be more amusing to rude minds, just opening to a taste of letters, than the fabulous story of the pagan gods, which is constantly interwoven in every piece of antient poetry. Hence the imitative arts of *sculpture, painting,* and *poetry,* were immediately employed in these pagan exhibitions. But this was not all. The first artists in every kind were of *Italy ;* and it was but natural for them to act these fables over again on the very spot that had first produced them. These too were the masters to the rest of *Europe.* So that *fashion* con-

[b] Alluding to a tract, so called, by GASCOIGNE, an attendant on the court, and poet of that time, who hath given us a narrative of the entertainments that passed on this occasion at *Kenelworth.*

curred

curred with the other prejudices of the time, to recommend this practice to the learned.

FROM the men of art and literature the enthusiasm spread itself to the great ; whose supreme delight it was to see the wonders of the old poetical story brought forth, and realized, as it were, before them [c]. And what, in truth, could they do better ? For, if I were not a little afraid of your raillery, I should desire to know what courtly amusements even of our time are comparable to the shows and masques, which were the delight and improvement of the court of ELIZABETH.

[c] Hence then it is that a celebrated dramatic writer of those days represents the entertainment of MASKS and SHOWS, as the highest indulgence that could be provided for a luxurious and happy monarch. His words are these;
"Music and poetry are his delight.
Therefore I'll have *Italian* masques by night,
Sweet speeches, comedies, and pleasing shows
And in the day, when he shall walk abroad,
Like SYLVAN NYMPHS, my pages shall be clad :
My men, like SATYRS, grazing on the lawns,
Shall with their goat-feet dance the antic hay :
Sometimes a lovely boy in DIAN'S shape,
With hair, that gilds the water as it glides,
Crownets of pearls about his naked arms,
And in his sportful hands an olive-tree,
Shall bathe him in a spring, and there hard-by
One like ACTÆON, peeping through the grove,
Shall by the angry Goddess be transform'd—
Such things as these best please his Majesty."
MARLOW'S Edward II.

I say, the *improvement*; for, besides that these shows were not in the number of the INERUDITÆ VOLUPTATES, so justly characterized and condemned by a wise antient, they were even highly useful and instructive. These devices, composed out of the poetical history, were not only the vehicles of compliment to the great on certain solemn occasions, but of the soundest moral lessons, which were artfully thrown in, and recommended to them by the charm of poetry and numbers. Nay, some of these masques were moral dramas in form, where the virtues and vices were impersonated. We know the cast of their composition by what we see of these fictions in the next reign ; and have reason to conceive of them with reverence when we find the names of FLETCHER and JONSON [*d*] to some of them. I say nothing of JONES and LAWES, though all the elegance of their respective arts was called in to assist the poet in the contrivance and execution of these entertainments.

AND, now the poets have fallen in my way, let me further observe, that the manifest superiority of this class of writers in ELIZABETH'S reign, and that of her successor, over all others who have succeeded to them, is, among other reasons, to be ascribed to the taste which then prevailed for these moral representations.

[*d*] Whom his friend Mr. SELDEN characterizeth in this manner,
"Omnia carmina doctus
Et calles mythων plasmata et historiam."
TIT. OF HON. p. 466.

This

This taught them to animate and impersonate every thing. Rude minds, you will say, naturally give into this practice. Without doubt. But art and genius do not disdain to cultivate and improve it. Hence it is, that we find in the phraseology and mode of thinking of that time, and of that time only, the essence of the truest and sublimest poetry.

WITHOUT doubt, Mr. ADDISON said, the poetry of that time is of a better taste than could well have been expected from its barbarism in other instances. But such prodigies as SHAKESPEAR and SPENSER would do great things in any age, and under every disadvantage.

MOST certainly they would, returned Dr. ARBUTH-NOT, but not the things that you admire so much in these immortal writers. And, if you will excuse the intermixture of a little philosophy in these ramblings, I will attempt to account for it.

THERE is, I think, in the revolutions of taste and language, a certain point, which is more favourable to the purposes of poetry, than any other. It may be difficult to fix this point with exactness. But we shall hardly mistake in supposing it lies somewhere between the rude essays of uncorrected fancy, on the one hand, and the refinements of reason and science, on the other.

AND such appears to have been the condition of our

and perspicuous, without affectation. At the same
time, the high figurative manner, which fits a language
so peculiarly for the uses of the poet, had not yet been
controlled by the prosaic genius of philosophy and
logic. Indeed, this character had been struck so
deeply into the *English* tongue, that it was not to be
removed by any ordinary improvements in either:
the reason of which might be, the delight which was
taken by the *English* very early in their old MYSTERIES
and MORALITIES; and the continuance of the same
spirit in succeeding times, by means of their MASQUES
and TRIUMPHS. And something like this, I observe,
attended the progress of the *Greek* and *Roman* poetry;
which was the *truest* poetry, on the clown's maxim in
SHAKESPEAR, because it was *the most feigning* [e]. It
had its rise, you know, like ours, from religion: and
pagan religion, of all others, was the properest to
introduce and encourage a spirit of allegory and moral
fiction. Hence we easily account for the allegoric cast
of their old dramas, which have a great resemblance
to our ancient moralities. NECESSITY is brought in as
a *person of the drama,* in one of ÆSCHYLUS's plays; and
DEATH in one of EURIPIDES: to say nothing of many
shadowy persons in the comedies of ARISTOPHANES.
The truth is, the pagan religion *deified* every thing,
and delivered these deities into the hand of their

[e] *Sacrifices,* says PLUTARCH, *without choruses and without
music, we have known: but for poetry, without fable and without
fiction, we know of no such thing.* Θυσίας μὲν ἀχόρους καὶ ἀναύλους
ἴσμεν· οὐκ ἴσμεν δὲ ἄμυθον οὐδὲ ἀψευδῆ ποίησιν. De aud. poët.
vol. i. p. 16.

painters,

painters, sculptors, and poets. In like manner, christian superstition, or, if you will, modern barbarism, *impersonated* every thing ; and these persons, in proper form, subsisted for some time on the stage, and almost to our days, in the masques. Hence the picturesque style of our old poetry ; which looks so fanciful in SPENSER, and which SHAKESPEAR's genius hath carried to the utmost sublimity.

I WILL not deny, said Mr. ADDISON, but there may be something in this deduction of the causes, by which you account for the strength and grandeur of the *English* poetry, unpolished as it still was in the hands of ELIZABETH's great poets. But for the masques themselves—

You forget, I believe, *one*, interrupted Dr. ARBUTHNOT, which does your favourite poet, MILTON, almost as much honour, as his *Paradise Lost.*—But I have no mind to engage in a further vindication of these fancies. I only conclude that the taste of the age, the state of letters, the genius of the *English* tongue, was such as gave a manliness to their compositions of all sorts, and even an elegance to those of the lighter forms, which we might do well to emulate, and not deride, in this æra of politeness.

BUT I am aware, as you say, I have been transported

times, awakened in us by the sight of this castle, that
what you object to is capable of a much fairer interpretation. You have a proof of it, in two or three
instances; in their festivals, their exercises, and their
poetical fictions: or, to express myself in the classical
forms, you have seen by this view of their CONVIVIAL,
GYMNASTIC, and MUSICAL character, that the times of
ELIZABETH may pass for golden, notwithstanding what
a fondness for this age of baser metal may incline us to
represent it.

In the mean time, these smaller matters have drawn
me aside from my main purpose. What surprised me
most, pursued he, was to hear you speak so slightly,
I would not call it by a worse name, of the GOVERNMENT
of ELIZABETH. Of the manners and tastes of different
ages, different persons, according to their views of things
will judge very differently. But plain facts speak so
strongly in favour of the policy of that reign, and the
superior talents of the sovereign, that I could not but
take it for the wantonness of opposition in you to
espouse the contrary opinion. And, now I am warmed
by this slight skirmish, I am even bold enough to dare
you to a defence of it; if, indeed, you were serious in
advancing that strange paradox. At least, I could
wish to hear upon what grounds you would justify so
severe an attack on the reverend administration of
that reign, supported by the wisdom of such men as
CECIL and WALSINGHAM, under the direction of so
accomplished a princess as our ELIZABETH. Your

manner

manner of defending even the wrong side of the question will, at least, be entertaining. And, I think, I may answer for our young friend, that his curiosity will lead him to join me in this request to you.

MR. ADDISON said, He did not expect to be called to so severe an account of what had escaped him on this subject. But, though I was ever so willing, continued he, to oblige you, this is no time or place for entering on such a controversy. We have not yet compleated the round of these buildings. And I would fain, methinks, make the circuit of that pleasant meadow. Besides its having been once, in another form, the scene of those shows you described so largely to us, it will deserve to be visited for the sake of the many fine views which, as we wind along it, we may promise to ourselves of these ruins.

You forget my bad legs, said Dr. ARBUTHNOT smiling; otherwise, I suppose, we can neither of us have any dislike to your proposal. But, as you please : let us descend from these heights. We may resume the conversation, as we walk along: and especially, as you propose, when we get down into that valley.

Facsimile of Title-page of the First Edition (black and red)

LETTERS

ON

CHIVALRY

AND

ROMANCE.

Guarda, che mal fato,
O giovenil vaghezza non ti meni
Al magazino de le ciancie. ah fuggi,
Fuggi quell incantato alloggiamento.
Quivi habitan le maghe, che incantando
Fan traveder, e traudir ciaſcuno.

TASSO.

LONDON:

L E T T E R S

O N

C H I V A L R Y

A N D

R O M A N C E:

Serving to illuſtrate ſome

Paſſages in the THIRD DIALOGUE.

Guarda, che mal fato
O giovenil vaghezza non ti meni
Al magazino de la ciancie, ab fuggi,
Fuggi quell incantato alloggiamento.
Quivi habitan le maghe, che incantande
Fan traveder, e traudir ciaſcuno.
                                        TASSO.

CONTENTS of the LETTERS.

LET-

LETTERS

ON

CHIVALRY.

LETTER I.

THE ages, we call barbarous, present us with many a subject of curious speculation. What, for instance, is more remarkable than the Gothic CHIVALRY? or than the spirit of ROMANCE,

as sings our philosophical bard ; but to come at this knowledge, is the difficulty. Sometimes a close attention to the workings of the human mind is sufficient to lead us to it : Sometimes more than that, the diligent observation of what passes without us, is necessary.

This last I take to be the case here. The prodigies, we are now contemplating, had their origin in the barbarous ages. Why then, says the fastidious modern, look any farther for the reason ? Why not resolve them at once into the usual caprice and absurdity of barbarians ?

This, you see, is a short and commodious philosophy. Yet barbarians have their *own*, such as it is, if they are not enlightened by our reason. 'Shall we then condemn them unheard, or will it not be fair to let them have the telling of their own story ?

Would we know, from what causes the institution of *Chivalry* was derived ? The time of its birth, the situation of the barbarians, amongst whom it arose, must be considered : their wants, designs, and policies must be explored : We must inquire when, and where, and how it came to pass that the western world became familiarized to this *Prodigy*, which we now start at.

Another thing is full as remarkable, and concerns us more nearly. The spirit of Chivalry, was a fire which soon spent itself ; But that of *Romance*, which was
kindled

kindled at it, burnt long, and continued its light and heat even to the politer ages.

The greatest geniuses of our own and foreign countries, such as Ariosto and Tasso in Italy, and Spenser and Milton in England, were seduced by these barbarities of their forefathers; were even charmed by the Gothic Romances. Was this caprice and absurdity in them? Or, may there not be something in the Gothic Romance peculiarly suited to the views of a genius, and to the ends of poetry? And may not the philosophic moderns have gone too far, in their perpetual ridicule and contempt of it?

To form a judgment in the case, the rise, progress, and genius of Gothic Chivalry must be explained.

The circumstances in the Gothic fictions and manners, which are proper to the ends of poetry (if any such there be) must be pointed out.

Reasons, for the decline and rejection of the Gothic taste in later times must be given.

You have in these particulars both the SUBJECT, and the PLAN of the following Letters.

LETTER II.

I Look upon Chivalry, as on some mighty River, which the fablings of the poets have made immortal. It may have sprung up amidst rude rocks, and blind deserts. But the noise and rapidity of its course, the extent of country it adorns, and the towns and palaces it ennobles, may lead a traveller out of his way and invite him to take a view of those dark caverns,

undè supernè
Plurimus Eridani per sylvam volvitur amnis.

I enter, without more words, on the subject I began to open to you in my last Letter.

The old inhabitants of these North-West parts of Europe were extremely given to the love and exercise of arms. The feats of Charlemagne and our Arthur, in particular, were so famous as in later times, when books of Chivalry were composed, to afford a principal subject to the writers of them.[1]

---

[1] Author's note in edition of 1788:—See a discourse at the end of *Love's Labour Lost* in Warb. Ed. of Shakespear; in which the *origin, subject,* and *character* of these books of Chivalry (or *Romances,* properly so called) are explained with an exactness of learning, and penetration, peculiar to that writer—
In tenui labor, at tenuis non gloria—

But

But CHIVALRY, properly so called, and under the idea "of a distinct military order, conferred in the way "of investiture, and accompanied with the solemnity "of an oath and other ceremonies, as described in "the old historians and romancers," was of later date, and seems to have sprung immediately out of the FEUDAL CONSTITUTION.

The FIRST and most sensible effect of this constitution, which brought about so mighty a change in the policies of Europe, was the erection of a prodigious number of petty tyrannies. For, though the great barons were closely tied to the service of their Prince by the conditions of their tenure, yet the power which was given them by it over their own numerous vassals was so great, that, in effect, they all set up for themselves ; affected an independency ; and were, in truth, a sort of absolute Sovereigns, at least with regard to one another. Hence, their mutual aims and interests often interfering, the feudal state was, in a good degree, a state of war : the feudal chiefs were in frequent enmity with each other : the several combinations of feudal tenants were so many separate armies under their head or chief : and their castles were so many fortresses, as well as palaces, of these puny princes.

In this state of things one sees, that all imaginable

according as the safety of these different communities, or the ambition of their leaders, might require. And this condition of the times, I suppose, gave rise to that military institution, which we know by the name of CHIVALRY.

FURTHER, there being little or no security to be had amidst so many restless spirits and the clashing views of a neighbouring numerous and independent nobility, the military discipline of their followers, even in the intervals of peace, was not to be relaxed, and their ardour suffered to grow cool by a total disuse of martial exercises. And hence the proper origin of JUSTS and TURNAMENTS; those images of war, which were kept up in the castles of the barons and, by an useful policy, converted into the amusement of the knights, when their arms were employed on no serious occasion.

I call this the *proper origin* of Justs and Turnaments; for the date of them is carried no higher, as far as I can find even in France (where unquestionably they made their first appearance) than the year 1066; which was not till after the introduction of the feudal government into that country. Soon after, indeed, we find them in England and in Germany; but not till the feudal policy had spread itself in those parts and had prepared the way for them.

You see, then, my notion is, that Chivalry was no absurd and freakish institution, but the natural and

even

even sober effect of the feudal policy ; whose turbulent genius breathed nothing but war, and was fierce and military even in its amusements.

I leave you to revolve this idea in your own mind. You will find, I believe, a reasonable foundation for it in the history of the feudal times, and in the spirit of the feudal government.

LETTER III.

IF the conjecture, I advanced, of the rise of Chivalry, from the circumstances of the feudal government, be thought reasonable, it will now be easy to account for the several CHARACTERISTICS of this singular profession.

I. " The passion for arms ; the spirit of enterprize ; " the honour of knighthood ; the rewards of valour ; " the splendour of equipages ; " in short, every thing that raises our ideas of the prowess, gallantry, and magnificence of these sons of Mars is naturally and easily explained on this supposition.

Ambition, interest, glory all concurred, under such circumstances, to produce these effects. The feudal

was given to the thoughts and passions of men, use and fashion would do the rest; and carry them to all the excesses of military fanaticism, which are painted so strongly, but scarcely exaggerated[1] in the old Romances.

[For instance, one of the strangest circumstances in those books, and which looks most like a mere extravagance of the imagination, is that of the *women-warriors*, with which they all abound. Butler in his Hudibras, who saw it in this light, ridicules it, as a most unnatural idea, with great spirit. Yet in this representation they did but copy from the manners of the times. Anna Comnena tells us, in the life of her father, that the wife of Robert the Norman fought side by side with her husband, in his battles; that she would rally the flying soldiers, and lead them back to the charge: And Nicetas observes that, in the time of Manuel Comnena, there were in one Crusade many women, armed like men, and on horseback.

What think you now of Tasso's Clorinda, whose prodigies of valour I dare say you have often laughed at? Or, rather, what think you of that constant pair,

"Gildippe, & Odoardo amanti e sposi,
"In valor d'arme, e in lealtà famosi?"

C. iii. S. 40.] *

[1] exaggerated,
* The paragraphs within brackets were not reprinted in this place in the edition of 1788. But compare Appendix H, pp. 169–170

"Their

II. " Their romantic ideas of justice ; their passion
" for adventures ; their eagerness to run to the succour
" of the distressed; and the pride they took in redressing
" wrongs, and removing grievances ; " All these distinguishing characters of genuine Chivalry are explained on the same principle. For, the feudal state
being a state of war, or rather of almost perpetual
violence, rapine, and plunder, it was unavoidable that,
in their constant skirmishes, stratagems, and surprizes,
numbers of the tenants or followers of one Baron
should be seized upon and carried away by the followers of another : And the interest, each had to
protect his own, would of course introduce the point of
honour in attempting by all means not only to retaliate
on the enemy, but to [1] rescue the captive sufferers out
of the hands of their oppressors.

It would be meritorious, in the highest degree, to
fly to their assistance, when they knew where they
were to be come at ; or to seek them out with diligence,
when they did not. This last service they called,[2]
Going in quest of adventures ; which at first, no doubt,
was confined to those of their own party, but afterwards, by the habit of acting on this principle, would
be extended much farther.[3] So that, in process of
time, we find the Knights errant, as they were now

[1] and, especially to
[2] This last feudal service soon introduced what may be truly
called *romantic*, the   [3] further

properly

properly styled, wandering the world over in search of occasions on which to exercise their generous, and disinterested valour,[1]

> Ecco quei, che le charte empion di sogni,
> Lancilotto, Tristano, e gli altri erranti.

III. " The courtesy, affability, and gallantry, for " which these adventurers were so famous, are but the " natural effects and consequences of their situation."

For the castles of the Barons were, as I said, the courts of these little sovereigns, as well as their fortresses; and the resort of their vassals thither, in honour of their chiefs, and for their own proper security, would make that civility and politeness, which is seen in courts and insensibly prevails there, a predominant part in the character of these assemblies.

This is the poet's own account of

> - - - - court and royal citadel,
> The great school-maistresse of all Courtesy.
>   B. III. C. vi. St. i.

And again, more largely in B. VI. C. i. S. I.

> Of Court it seems men Courtesie doe call,
> For that it there most useth to abound;

---

[1] valour, indifferently to friends and enemies in distress;

And

And well beseemeth that in Princes hall
That Virtue should be plentifully found,
Which of all goodly manners is the ground
And roote of civil conversation :
Right so in *faery court* it did resound,
Where courteous knights and ladies most did won
Of all on earth, and made a matchless paragon.

For *Faery Court* means the *reign of Chivalry* ; which, it seems, had undergone a fatal revolution before the age of Milton, who tells us that *Courtesy*

- - - is sooner found in lonely sheds
With smoaky rafters, than in tap'stry halls
And courts of princes, where it first was nam'd,
And yet is most pretended.   MASK.

Further, The free commerce of the ladies, in those knots and circles of the great, would operate so far on the sturdiest knights as to give birth to the attentions of gallantry. But this gallantry would take a refined turn, not only from the necessity there was of maintaining the strict forms of decorum, amidst a promiscuous conversation under the eye of the Prince and in his own family ; but also from the inflamed sense they must needs have of the frequent outrages committed, by their neighbouring clans of adversaries, on the honour of the Sex, when by chance of war they had fallen into their hands. Violations of chastity being

others, the fairest and strongest claim of the sex itself
to such protection, it is no wonder that the notions of
it were, in time, carried to so platonic an elevation.

Thus, again, the great master of Chivalry himself,
on this subject,

> It hath been thro' all ages ever seen,
>   That, with the praise of arms and chivalry,
> The prize of beauty still hath joined been;
>   And that for reason's special privity:
> For either doth on other much rely;
>   For HE mee seems most fit the fair to serve,
> That can her best defend from villany;
>   And SHE most fit his service doth deserve,
> That fairest is, and from her faith will never swerve.
>   SPENSER B. iv. c. v.

Not but the foundation of this refined gallantry was
laid in the antient manners of the German nations.
Cæsar tells us how far they carried their practice of
chastity, which he seems willing to account for on
political principles. However that be, their consideration of the sex was prodigious, as we see in the
history of their irruptions into the Empire; where,
among all their ravages and devastations of other sorts,
we find they religiously abstained from offering any
violence to the honour of the women.

IV. It only remains to account for that " character
" of Religion," which was so deeply imprinted on the
minds of all knights and was essential to their institution.

tion. We are even told, that *the love of God and of the Ladies* went hand in hand, in the duties and ritual of Chivalry.

Two reasons may be assigned for this singularity,

First, the superstition of the Times, in which Chivalry arose ; which was so great that no institution of a public nature could have found credit in the world, that was not consecrated by the Churchmen, and closely interwoven with religion.

Secondly, the condition of the Christian world ;[1] which had been harrassed by long wars, and had but just recovered a breathing-time from the brutal ravages of the Saracen armies. The remembrance of what they had lately suffered from these grand enemies of the faith, made it natural and even necessary[2] to engage a new military order on the side of religion.

And how warmly this principle, *a zeal for the faith*, was acted upon by the professors of Chivalry, and how deeply it entered into their ideas of the military Character, we see from the term so constantly used by the old Romancers, of RECREANT[3] Knight; by which they meant to express, with the utmost force, their disdain of a dastard or vanquished knight. For[4] many such of them as had not imbibed the full Spirit of their profession, were induced to renounce their faith, in order to regain their liberty. These men, as sinning against the great fundamental laws of Chivalry, they branded with this name; a name of complicated reproach, which implied a want of the two most essential qualities of a Knight, COURAGE and FAITH.

And here, by the way,[1] the reason appears why the Spaniards, of all the Europeans, were furthest gone in every characteristic madness of true chivalry. To all the other considerations, here mentioned, their fanaticism in every way was especially instigated and kept alive by the memory and neighbourhood of their old infidel invaders.

And thus we seem to have a fair account of that PROWESS, GENEROSITY, GALANTRY, and RELIGION, which were the peculiar and vaunted characteristics of the purer ages of Chivalry.

Such was the state of things in the western World, when the crusades to the holy land were set on foot. Whence we see how well prepared the minds of men were for engaging in that enterprize. Every object, that had entered into the views of the institutors of chivalry, and had been followed by it's professors, was now at hand[2] to inflame the military and religious ardor of the knights, to the utmost. And here, in

[1] Hence too   [2] hand,

fact,

fact, we find the strongest and boldest features of their genuine character : *Daring* to madness, in enterprizes of hazard : Burning with zeal for the delivery of the *oppressed* ; and, which was deemed the height of *religious* merit, for the rescue of the holy city out of the hands of infidels : And, lastly exalting their honour of *chastity* so high as to profess celibacy ; as they constantly did, in the several orders of knighthood created on that extravagant occasion.

LETTER IV.

WHAT think you, my good friend, of my last learned Letter ? [1] Don't you begin to favour this [2] conjecture, as whimsical as it may [3] seem, of *the rise and genius* of knight-errantry ?

But you ask me, where I learned the several particulars, on which I form this profound system. [4] You are willing, I perceive, [5] to advance on sure grounds ; and call [6] upon me to point out to you the authorities, from which I pretend to have collected the several marks and characteristics of true chivalry.

Your request is reasonable, and I acknowledge the omission [7] in not acquainting you that my information—

was taken from it's proper Source, the *old Romances*
Not that I shall make a merit with you in havin
perused these barbarous volumes my self; much les
would I impose the ungrateful task upon you. Thank
to the curiosity of certain painful collectors, this know
ledge may be obtained at a cheaper rate. And I thin
it sufficient to refer you to a learned and very elaborat
Memoir of a French writer, who has put together a
that is requisite to be known on this subject. Material
are first laid in, before the Architect goes to work
and if the structure, I am here raising out of them, b
to your mind, you will not think the worse of it becaus
I [1] pretend not, myself, to have worked in the quarr
In a word, and to drop this magnificent allusion, i
I account to you for the rise and genius of chivalry, i
is all you are to expect : For an idea of what chivalr
was in itself, you may have recourse to the xx tom
of the *Memoirs of the Academy of Inscriptions and bell
Lettres*

And with this explanation I return to my prope
business

Supposing my idea of chivalry to be fairly given, th
conjecture I advance on the *origin and nature* of it, yo
incline to think, may deserve to be admitted. But yo
may,[2] perhaps, admit it the more readily, if you reflec
" That there is a remarkable correspondency betwee
" the manners of the old heroic times, as painted b

---

[1] to tom. xx   [2] will

" thei

" their great romancer, Homer, and those which are
" represented to us in the books [1] of modern knight-
" errantry." A fact, of which no good account, I
believe, can be given but by the assistance of another,
not less certain, " That the political state of Greece,
" in the earlier periods of it's story, was similar in many
" respects to that of Europe, as broken by the feudal
" system into an infinite number of petty independent
" governments."

It is not my design to encroach on the province of
the learned person [a], to whom I owe this hint, and
who hath undertaken, at his leisure, to enlarge upon it.
But some few circumstances of agreement between the
heroic and *gothic* manners, such as are most obvious and
occur to my memory, while I am writing, may be worth
putting down, by way of specimen only of what may
be expected from a professed inquiry into this curious
subject.

And, FIRST, " the military enthusiasm of the Barons
" is but of a piece with the fanaticism of the Heroes."
Hence the same particularity of description in the
account of battles, wounds, deaths in the Greek poet,
as in the gothic romancers. Hence that perpetual
succession of combats and deeds of arms, even to
satiety, in the Iliad : And hence that minute curiosity [2]

[1] in books
[a] See the Memoir, just quoted.
[2] curiosity,

in

in the display of their [1] dresses, arms, accoutrements,[2] which appears [3] so strange, in that poem. The minds of all men, being occupied and in a manner possessed with warlike images and ideas, were much gratified by the poet's dwelling on the very slightest circumstances of these things ; [4] which now, for want of their prejudices, appear cold and unaffecting to modern readers.

But the correspondency holds in more particular considerations. For [5]

2. " We hear much of Knights-errant encountering " *Giants,* and quelling *Savages,* in books of chivalry."

These Giants were oppressive feudal Lords,[6] and every Lord was to be met with, like the Giant, in his strong hold, or castle. Their dependants of a lower form, who imitated the violence of their superiors, and had not their castles, but their lurking-places, were the Savages of Romance. The greater Lord was called a Giant, for his power ; the less, a Savage, for his brutality.

All this is shadowed out in the gothic tales, and sometimes expressed in plain words. The objects of the knight's vengeance go indeed by the various names

---

[1] the	[2] accoutrements of the combatants
[3] we find	[4] things,
[5] For,	[6] Lords ;

of Giants, Paynims, Saracens and Savages. But of what family they all are, is clearly seen from the Poet's description.[1]

> What Mister wight, quoth he, and how far hence
>   Is he, that doth to travellers such harms ?
> He is, said he, a man of great defence,
>   Expert in battle, and in deeds of arms ;
>   And more embolden'd by the wicked charms
> With which his daughter doth him still support ;
>   Having *great Lordships got and goodly farms*
> *Thro' strong oppression of his pow'r* [2] *extort ;*
> By which he still them holds and keeps with strong effort:
>
> And daily he his wrong encreaseth more :
>   For never wight he lets to pass that way
> Over his bridge, albee he rich or poor,
>   But he him makes his passage-penny pay :
>   Else he doth hold him back or beat away.
> Thereto he hath a *Groom of evil Guise*
>   Whose scalp is bare that bondage doth bewray,
> Which polls and pills the poor in piteous wise,
> But he himself upon the rich doth tyrannize.
>
>   SPENSER, B. v. C. 2.

Here we have the great oppressive Baron very graphically set forth : And the *Groom of evil guise* is as plainly the Baron's vassal. The romancers, we see, took no great liberty with these respectable personages, when they called the one a Giant, and the other a Savage.

"Another terror of the gothic ages was, *Monsters*,
"*Dragons*, and *Serpents*." These stories were received
in those days for several reasons : 1. From the vulgar
belief of enchantments : 2. From their being reported
on the faith of Eastern tradition, by the adventurers
into the holy land : 3. In still later times, from the
strange things told and believed, on the discovery of
the new world.

This last consideration we find employed by Spenser
to give an air of probability to his Faery tales, in the
preface to his second book.

Now in all these respects Greek antiquity very much
resembles the Gothic. For what are Homer's Læstri-
gons, and Cyclops, but bands of lawless savages, with,
each of them, a Giant of enormous size at their head ?
And what are the Grecian Bacchus, Hercules, and
Theseus but Knights-errant,[1] the exact counter-parts
of Sir Launcelot and Amadis de Gaule ?

For this interpretation we have the authority of our
great Poet.

> Such first was BACCHUS, that with furious might
> All th'East, before untam'd, did overcome,
> And wrong repressed and establish'd right,
> Which lawless men had formerly fordonne.

[1] and Hercules, but knights-errant,

Next

Next HERCULES his like ensample shew'd,
  Who all the West with equal conquest wonne,
  And monstrous tyrants with his club subdu'd,
The club of justice drad, with kingly pow'r endu'd.

B. v. C. 1.[1]

Nay, could the very castle of a Gothic giant be better described than in the words of Homer,

High walls and battlements the courts inclose,
And the strong gates defy a host of foes.

Od. B. xvii. ver. 318.

And do not you remember that the Grecian worthies were, in their day, as famous for encountering Dragons and quelling Monsters of all sorts, as for suppressing Giants ?

——per hos cecidere justâ
Morte Centauri, cecidit tremendæ
Flamma Chimæræ.

3. " The oppressions, which it was the glory of the Knight to avenge, were frequently carried on, as we are told, *by the charms and enchantments of women.*"

These *charms*, we may suppose, are often meta-

selves. Sometimes they are taken to be real; the ignorance of those ages acquiescing in such conceits.

And are not these stories matched by those of Calypso and Circe, the enchantresses of the Greek poet?

Still there are conformities more directly to our purpose.

4. "Robbery and Pyracy were honourable in both; so far were they from reflecting any discredit on the antient or modern *redressers of wrongs*."

What account can be given of this,[1] but that, in the feudal times and in the early days of Greece, when government was weak and unable to redress the frequent injuries of petty sovereigns, it would be glorious for private adventurers' to undertake this work; and, if they could accomplish it in no other way, to pay them in kind by downright plunder and rapine?

This in effect is the account given us, of the same disposition of the old Germans, by Cæsar. "Latro-cinia, says he, nullam habent infamiam, quæ extra fines cujusque civitatis fiunt." And the reason appears from what he had just told us—in pace, nullus est communis magistratus; sed principes regionum atque

---

[1] this odd circumstance,

pagorum

pagorum inter suos jus dicunt, controversiasque minuunt." *De bello Gall.* 1. vi. § 21.

5. Their manners, in another respect, were the same. " Bastardy was in credit with both." They were extremely watchful over the chastity of their own women ; but such as they could seize upon in the enemy's quarter,[1] were lawful prize. Or, if at any time they transgressed in this sort at home, the heroic ages were complaisant enough to cover the fault by an ingenious fiction. The offspring was reputed divine.

Nay, so far did they carry their indulgence to this commerce, that their greatest heroes were the fruit of Goddesses approached by mortals ; just as we hear of the doughtiest knights being born of Fairies.

6. Is it not strange, that, together with the greatest fierceness and savageness of character, " The utmost generosity, hospitality, and courtesy should be imputed to the heroic ages ? " Achilles was at once the most relentless, vindictive, implacable, and the friendliest of men.

We have the very same representation in the Gothic Romances, where it is almost true what Butler says humorously of these benign heroes, that

How are these contradictions [1] to be reconciled [2] but by observing, that,[3] as in those lawless times dangers and distresses of all sorts abounded, there would be the same demand for compassion, gentleness, and generous attachments to the unfortunate, those especially of their own clan, as of resentment, rage, and animosity against their enemies ?

7. Again: Consider the martial *Games,* which antient Greece delighted to celebrate on great and solemn occasions : And see if they had not the same origin, and the same purpose, as the *Tournaments* of the Gothic warriors.

8. Lastly, " the passion for adventures, so natural in their situation, would be as naturally attended with the love of praise and glory."

Hence the same encouragement, in the old Greek and Gothic times, to panegyrists and poets ; the BARDS being as welcome to the tables of the feudal lords, as the AOIΔOI of old, to those of the Grecian heroes.

And, as the same causes ever produce the same effects, we find that, even so late as Elizabeth's reign, the savage Irish (who were much in the state of the antient Greeks, living under the anarchy, rather than govern-

---

[1] contradictions, in the characters of the antient and modern men of arms,

[2] reconciled,   [3] obserfing that,

ment,

Rhymers in principal estimation. It was for the reason just given, for the honour of their panegyrics on their fierce adventures and successes. And thus it was in Greece.

For chief to Poets such respect belongs
By rival nations courted for their Songs;
These, states invite, and mighty kings admire
Wide as the Sun displays his vital fire.

Od. B. xvii.

L E T T E R V.

THE purpose of the casual hints, suggested in my last letter, was only to shew that the resemblance between the heroic and Gothic ages is very great.[1] And tho' you say true, that ignorance and barbarity itself might account for some circumstances of this resemblance, yet the parallel would hardly have held so long, and run so closely, if the *civil* condition of both had not been much the same.

So that when we see a sort of chivalry springing up among the Greeks, who were confessedly in a state resembling that of the feudal barons, and attended by the like symptoms and effects, is it not fair to conclude that the chivalry of the Gothic times was owing to that common corresponding *state*, and received it's character from it ?

And this circumstance, by the way, accounts for the constant mixture, which the modern critic esteems so monstrous, of pagan fable with the fairy tales of Romance. The passion for antient learning, just then revived, might seduce the classic poets, such as Spenser and Tasso, for instance, into this practice ; but the similar turn and genius of antient manners and of the fictions founded upon them, would make it appear easy and natural in all.

I am aware, as you object to me, that, in the affair of *Religion* and *Gallantry,* the resemblance between the hero and knight is not so striking.

But the religious character of the knight was an accident of the times, and no proper effect of his *civil* condition.

And that his devotion for the sex should so far surpass that of the hero, is a fresh confirmation of my system.

For, tho' much, no doubt, might be owing to the different humour and genius of the East and West, antecedent to any custom[1] and forms of government, and independent of them, yet the consideration had

[1] customs

of

of the females in the feudal constitution will, of itself, account for this difference. It made them capable of succeeding to fiefs as well as the men. And does not one see, on the instant, what respect and dependence this privilege would draw upon them ?

It was of mighty consequence who should obtain the grace of a rich heiress. And tho', in the strict feudal times, she was supposed to be in the power and disposal of her superior Lord, yet this rigid state of things did not last long ; and, while it did last, could not abate much of the homage that would be paid to the fair feudatary.

Thus, when interest had begun the habit, the language of love and flattery would soon do the rest. And to what that language tended you may see by the constant strain of the Romances themselves. Some distressed damsel was the spring and mover of every knight's adventure. She was to be rescued by his arms, or won by the fame and admiration of his prowess.

The plain meaning of all which was this : That, as in those turbulent feudal times a protector was necessary to the weakness of the sex, so the courteous and valorous knight was to approve himself fully qualified for that office. And we find, he had other motives to set him on work than the mere charms and graces, tho' ever so bewiching,[1] of the person addressed.

Hence then, as I suppose, the custom was introduced : And, when introduced, you will hardly wonder it should operate much longer and farther [1] than the reason may seem to require, on which it was founded.[2]

In conclusion of this topic [3] I must just observe to you, that the two poems of Homer express in the liveliest manner, and were intended to expose, the capital mischiefs and inconveniences arising from the *political state* of old Greece : The Iliad, the dissensions that naturally spring up amongst a number of independent chiefs ; And the Odyssey, the insolence of their greater subjects, more especially when unrestrained by the presence of their Sovereign.

These were the subjects of his pen. And can any thing more exactly resemble the condition of the *feudal times*, when, on occasion of any great enterprize, as that of the Crusades, the designs of the confederate Christian states were perpetually frustrated, or interrupted at least, by the dissensions of their leaders ; and their affairs at home as perpetually distressed and disordered by the rebellious usurpations [4] of their greater vassals ? [5]

So that Jerusalem [6] was to the European, what

---

[1] further
[2] For an additional passage in the 1788 edition see Appendix D.
[3] topic,
[4] by domestic license, and the rebellious usurpations
[5] For an additional passage in the 1788 edition see Appendix E.
[6] So that, in all respects, *Jerusalem*

Troy

Troy had been to the Grecian Princes.[1] And you will now, I believe, not be supprized to find that Tasso's immortal poem was planned after the model of the Iliad.[2]

LETTER VI

LET it be no surprize [3] to you that, in the close of my last Letter, I presumed to bring the *Gierusalemme liberata* into competition with the Iliad.

So far as the heroic and Gothic manners are the same, the pictures of each, if well taken, must be equally entertaining. But I go further, and maintain that the circumstances, in which they differ, are clearly to the advantage of the Gothic designers.

You see, my purpose is to lead you from this forgotten chivalry to a more amusing subject, I mean [4] the *Poetry* we still read, and which [5] was founded upon it.

Much has been said, and with great truth, of the felicity of Homer's age, for poetical manners. But as Homer was a citizen of the world, when he had seen in Greece, on the one hand, the manners he has described, could he, on the other hand, have seen in the west the

[1] heroes

manners of the feudal ages, I make no doubt but he would certainly have preferred the latter. And the grounds of this preference would, I suppose, have been " *The improved gallantry of the feudal times* [1]; and the " *superior solemnity of their superstitions.*"

If any great poet, like Homer, had lived amongst, and sung of, the Gothic knights (for after all [2] Spenser and Tasso came too late, and it was impossible for them to paint truly and perfectly what was no longer seen or believed) this preference, I persuade myself, had been very sensible. But their fortune was not so happy.

—omnes illacrymabiles
Urgentur, ignotique longâ
Nocte, carent quia vate sacro.

As it is, we may take a guess of what the subject was capable of affording to real genius from the rude sketches we have of it, in the old Romancers. And it is but looking into any of them to be convinced that the *gallantry*, which inspirited [3] the feudal times, was of a nature to furnish the poet with finer scenes and subjects of description in every view, than the simple and uncontrolled barbarity of the Grecian.

The principal entertainment arising from the delineation of these consists in the exercise of the

[1] Gothic knights
[2] had flourished in these times and given the feudal **manners** from the *life* (for, after all,

[3] inspired

boisterous

boisterous passions, which are provoked and kept alive from one end of the Iliad to the other, by every imaginable scene of rage, revenge, and slaughter. In the other, together with these, the gentler and more humane affections are awakened in us by the most interesting displays of love and friendship ; of love, elevated to it's noblest heights ; and of friendship, operating on the purest motives. The mere variety of these paintings is a relief to the reader, as well as writer. But their beauty, novelty, and pathos give them a vast advantage, on the comparison.

[Consider, withall, the surprizes, accidents, adventures which probably and naturally attend on the life of wandering knights ; the occasion there must be for describing the wonders of different countries, and of presenting to view the manners and policies of distant states : all which make so conspicuous a part of the materials of the greater poetry.[1]]

So that, on the whole, tho' the spirit, passions, rapin,[2] and violence of the two sets of manners were equal, yet there was a dignity, a magnificence, a variety [3] in the feudal, which the other wanted.

As to *religious machinery*, perhaps the popular system of each was equally remote from reason,[4] yet the latter had something in it more amusing, as well as more awakening to the imagination.

The current popular tales of Elves and Fairies were even fitter to take the credulous mind, and charm it into a willing admiration of the *specious miracles,* which[1] wayward fancy delights in, than those of the old traditionary rabble of pagan divinities. And then, for the more solemn fancies of witchcraft and incantation, the horrors of[2] the Gothic were[3] above measure striking and terrible. [The mummeries of the pagan priests were childish, but the Gothic Enchanters shook and alarmed all nature.][4]

[5] We feel this difference very sensibly in reading the antient and modern poets. You would not compare the Canidia of Horace with the Witches in Macbeth. And what are Virgil's myrtles dropping blood, to Tasso's enchanted forest ?

Ovid indeed, who had a fancy turn'd to romance, makes Medea, in a rant, talk wildly. But was this the common language of their other writers ? The enchantress in Virgil says cooly of the very chiefest prodigies of her charms and poisons,

[1] *specious miracles* which
[2] " the horrors of " not in the 1788 edition.
[3] are
[4] The sentence : ' The mummeries . . . nature ' is omitted in the 1788 edition.
[5] For the different reading of the following passage, down to ' in this place ', p. 113, in the 1788 edition, see Appendix F.

His

His ego sæpè lupum fieri, & se condere sylvis
Mœrin ; sæpè animas imis excire sepulchris,
Atque satas alio vidi traducere messes.

The admirable poet has given an air of the marvellous to his subject, by the magic of his expression.
Else, what do we find here, but the ordinary effects of
melancholy, the vulgar superstition of *evoking Spirits*,
and the supposed influence of *fascination* on the hopes
of rural industry.

Non isthic obliquo oculo mihi commoda quisquam
    Limat . . .

says the poet of his country-seat, as if this security
from a *fascinating Eye* were a singular privilege, and
the mark of a more than common good fortune.

Shakespear, on the other hand, with a terrible
sublime (which not so much the energy of his genius,
as the nature of his subject drew from him) gives us
another idea of the *rough magic*, as he calls it, of fairy
enchantment.

                            . . . I have bedimm'd
The noon-tide Sun, call'd forth the mutinous winds,
And 'twixt the green sea and the azure vault
Set roaring war ; to the dread rattling thunder
Have I giv'n fire, and rifted Jove's stout oak
With his own bolt : The strong-bas'd promontory
Have I made shake, and by the spurrs pluck'd up
The Pine and Cedar : Graves, at my command,
Have open'd, and let forth their sleepers . . .

                                    The

The last circumstance, you will say, is but the *animas imis excire sepulchris* of the latin poet. But a very significant word marks the difference. The pagan necromancers had a hundred little tricks by which they pretended to call up the ghosts, or shadows of the dead : but these, in the ideas of paganism, were quite another thing from Shakespear's *Sleepers*.

This may serve for a cast of Shakespear's magic : And I can't but think that, when Milton wanted to paint the horrors of that night (one of the noblest parts in his *Paradise Regained*) which the Devil himself is feigned to conjure up in the wilderness, the Gothic language and ideas helped him to work up his tempest with such terror. You will judge from these lines :

> . . . nor staid the terror there ;
> Infernal ghosts and hellish furies round
> Environ'd ; some howl'd, some yell'd, some shriek'd,
> Some bent at thee their fiery darts . . .

But above all from the following,

> Thus pass'd the night so foul, till morning fair
> Came forth with pilgrim steps in amice gray,
> Who with her *radiant finger* still'd the roar
> Of thunder, chas'd the clouds, and laid the winds
> And *griesly specters* . . .

Where the *radiant finger* points at the potent wand of the Gothic magicians, which could reduce the calm

of

of nature, upon occasion, as well as disturb it ; and the *griesly specters laid* by the approach of morn, were apparently of their raising, as a sagacious critic perceived when he took notice " how very injudicious it " was to retail the *popular superstition* in this place [*e*]."

After [1] all, the conclusion is not to be drawn so much from particular passages, as from the *general impression* left on our minds in reading the antient and modern poets. And this is so much in favour of the *Latter*, that Mr. Addison scruples not to say, " The Antients " have not much of this poetry among them ; for, " indeed (continues he) almost the whole substance of " it owes it's original to the darkness and superstition " of later ages—Our forefathers looked upon nature with " more reverence and horror, before the world was " enlightened by learning and philosophy, and loved " to astonish themselves with the apprehensions of " Witchcraft, Prodigies, Charms, and Inchantments. " There was not a village in England, that had not a " Ghost in it,[2] the churchyards were all haunted,[3] every " large common had a circle of fairies belonging to it,[4] " and there was scarce a Shepherd to be met with who " had not seen a spirit."

We are upon enchanted ground, my friend ; and you are to think yourself well used that I detain you no

rest. And without more words you will readily apprehend that the fancies of our modern bards are not only more gallant, but, on a change of the scene, more sublime, more terrible, more alarming, than those of the classic fablers. In a word, you will find that the *manners* they paint, and the *superstitions* they adopt, are the more poetical for being Gothic.

LETTER VII.

BUT nothing shews the difference of the two systems under consideration more plainly, than the effect they really had on the two greatest of our Poets; at least the Two which an English reader is most fond to compare with Homer,[1] I mean SPENSER and MILTON.

It is not to be doubted but that each of these bards had kindled his poetic fire from classic fables. So that, of course, their prejudices would lie that way. Yet they both appear, when most inflamed, to have been more particularly rapt with the Gothic fables of chivalry.

Spenser, tho' he had been long nourished with the spirit and substance of Homer and Virgil, chose the times of chivalry for his theme, and fairy Land for the scene of his fictions. He could have planned, no doubt, an heroic design on the exact classic model : Or, he might have trimmed between the Gothic and Classic,

---

[1] Homer

as his contemporary Tasso did. But the charms of
fairy prevailed. And if any think, he was seduced by
Ariosto into this choice, they should consider that it
could be only for the sake of his subject ; for the genius
and character of these poets was widely different.

Under this idea then of a Gothic, not classical poem,
the *Faery Queen* is to be read and criticized. And on
these principles, it would not be difficult to unfold its
merit in another way than has been hitherto attempted.

Milton, it is true, preferred the classic model to the
Gothic. But it was after long hesitation ; and his
favourite subject was *Arthur and his Knights of the
round table*. On this he had fixed for the greater part
of his life. What led him to change his mind was,
partly, as I suppose, his growing fanaticism ;[1] partly,
his ambition to take a different rout from Spenser ;
but chiefly perhaps, the discredit into which the stories
of chivalry had now fallen by the immortal satire of
Cervantes. Yet we see thro' all his poetry, where his
enthusiasm flames out most, a certain predilection for
the legends of chivalry before the fables of Greece.

This circumstance, you know, has given offence to
the austerer and more mechanical critics. They are
ready to censure his judgment, as juvenile and un-

imagine that Milton did not perceive the defects of
these works, as well as they? No: it was not the
composition of books of chivalry, but the *manners*
described in them, that took his fancy; as appears
from his *Allegro*—

> Towred cities please us then
> And the busy hum of men,
> Where throngs of knights and barons bold
> In weeds of peace high triumphs hold,
> With store of ladies, whose bright eyes
> Rain influence, and judge the prize
> Of wit, or arms, while both contend
> To win her grace, whom all commend.

And when in the *Penseroso* he draws, by a fine contrivance, the same kind of image to sooth melancholy
which he had before given to excite mirth, he indeed
extolls an *author* of one of these [1] romances, as he had
before, in general, extolled the *subject* of them; but it is
an author [2] worthy of his praise; not the writer of
Amadis, or [3] *Sir Launcelot of the Lake*, but Chaucer
himself,[4] who has left an unfinished story on the
Gothic or feudal model.

> Or, call up him that left half-told
> The story of Cambuscan bold,
> Of Camball and of Algarsife,
> And who had Canace to wife

[1] an *author*, or two, of these
[2] they are authors   [3] and
[4] ; but Fairy SPENSER and CHAUCER himself,

                                                      That

That own'd the virtuous ring and glass,
And of the wondrous horse of brass,
On which the Tartar king did ride;
And if ought else great bards beside
In sage and solemn tunes have sung
Of turneys and of trophies hung,
Of forests and inchantments drear,
Where more is meant than meets the ear.

The conduct then of these two poets may incline us to think with more respect, than is commonly done of the *Gothic manners*, I mean[1] as adapted to the uses of the greater poetry.

I say [2] nothing of Shakespear,[3] because the sublimity (the divinity, let it be, if nothing else will serve) of his genius kept no certain rout, but rambled at hazard into all the regions of human life and manners. So that we can hardly say what he preferred, or what he rejected, on full deliberation. Yet one thing is clear, that even he is greater when he uses Gothic manners and machinery, than when he employs classical: which brings us again to the same point, that the former have, by their nature and genius, the advantage of the latter in producing the *sublime*.

[1] manners; I mean,
[2] shall add
[3] to what I before observed of SHAKESPEAR,

LETTER VIII.

I spoke "of criticizing Spenser's poem, under the "idea, not of a classical but Gothic composition."

It is certain much light might be thrown on that singular work, were an able critic to consider it in this view. For instance, he might go some way towards explaining, perhaps justifying, the general plan and *conduct* of the Faery[1] Queen, which, to classical readers has appeared indefensible.

I have taken the fancy, with your leave, to try my hand on this curious subject.

When an architect examines a Gothic structure by Grecian rules, he finds nothing but deformity. But the Gothic architecture has it's own rules, by which when it comes to be examined, it is seen to have it's merit, as well as the Grecian. The question is not, which of the two is conducted in the simplest or truest taste: but, whether there be not sense and design in both, when scrutinized by the laws on which each is projected.

The same observation holds of the two sorts of poetry. Judge of the *Faery Queen* by the classic models, and you are shocked with it's disorder: consider it with an eye to it's Gothic original, and you find it

---

[1] Fairy (and so throughout : Ed.)

regular.

regular. The unity and simplicity of the former are more complete : but the latter has that sort of unity and simplicity, which results from it's nature.

The Faery Queen then, as a Gothic poem, derives it's METHOD, as well as the other characters of it's composition, from the established modes and ideas of chivalry.

It was usual, in the days of knight-errantry, at the holding of any great feast, for Knights to appear before the Prince, who presided at it, and claim the privilege of being sent on any adventure, to which the solemnity might give occasion. For it was supposed that, when such a *throng of knights and barons bold,* as Milton speaks of, were got together, the distressed would flock in from all quarters, as to a place where they knew they might find and claim redress for all their grievances.

This was the real practice, in the days of pure and antient chivalry. And an image of this practice was afterwards kept up in the castles of the great, on any extraordinary festival or solemnity : of which, if you want an instance, I refer you to the description of a feast made at Lisle in 1453, in the court of Philip the Good, Duke of Burgundy,[1] for a crusade against the Turks : As you may find it given at large in the memoirs of *Matthieu de Conci, Olivier de la Marche,* and

That feast was held for *twelve* days : and each day was distinguished by the claim and allowance of some adventure.

Now laying down this practice, as a foundation for the poet's design, you will see how properly the *Faery Queen* is conducted.

——" I devise, says the poet himself in his Letter " to Sir W. Raleigh, that the Faery Queen kept her " annual feaste xii days : upon which xii several days, " the occasions of the xii several adventures hapened ; " which being undertaken by xii several knights, are " in these xii books severally handled."

Here you have the poet delivering his own method, and the reason of it. It arose out of the order of his subject. And would you desire a better reason for his choice ?

Yes ; you will say, a poet's method is not that of his subject. I grant you, as to the order of *time,* in which the recital is made ; for here, as Spenser observes (and his own practice agrees to the Rule) lies the main difference between *the poet historical, and the historio-grapher* : The reason of which is drawn from the nature of Epic composition itself, and holds equally, let the subject be what it will, and whatever the system of manners be, on which it is conducted. Gothic or Classic makes no difference in this respect.

But

But the case is not the same with regard to the general plan of a work, or what may be called the order of *distribution*, which is and must be governed by the subject-matter itself. It was as requisite for the Faery Queen to consist of the adventures of twelve knights, as for the Odyssey to be confined to the adventures of one Hero : Justice had otherwise not been done to his subject.

So that if you will say any thing against the poet's method, you must say that he should not have chosen this subject. But this objection arises from your classic ideas of Unity, which have no place here ; and are in every view foreign to the purpose, if the poet has found means to give his work, tho' consisting of many parts, the advantage of Unity. For in some reasonable sense or other, it is agreed, every work of art must be *one*, the very idea of a work requiring it.

If you ask then, what is this *Unity* of Spenser's Poem ? I say, It consists in the relation of it's several adventures to one common *original*, the appointment of the Faery Queen ; and to one common *end*, the completion of the Faery Queen's injunctions. The knights issued forth on their adventures on the breaking up of this annual feast ; and the next annual feast, we are to suppose, is to bring them together again from the

This, it is true, is not the classic Unity, which consists in the representation of one entire action : but it is an Unity of another sort, an unity resulting from the respect which a number of related actions have to one common purpose. In other words, It is an unity of *design*, and not of action.

This Gothic method of design in poetry may be, in some sort, illustrated by what is called the Gothic method of design in Gardening. A wood or grove cut out into many separate avenues or glades was amongst the most favourite of the works of art, which our fathers attempted in this species of cultivation. These walks were distinct from each other, had, each, their several destination, and terminated on their own proper objects. Yet the whole was brought together and considered under one view by the relation which these various openings had, not to each other, but to their common and concurrent center. You and I are, perhaps, agreed that this sort of gardening is not of so true a taste as that which *Kent and Nature* have brought us acquainted with ; where the supreme art of the Designer consists in disposing his ground and object into an *entire landskip* ; and grouping them, if I may use the term, in so easy a manner, that the careless observer, tho' he be taken with the symmetry of the whole, discovers no art in the combination :

> In lieto aspetto il bel giardin s'aperse,
> Acque stagnanti, mobili cristalli,

Fior

Fior vari, e varie piante, herbe diverse,
Apriche Collinette, ombrose valli,
Selve, e spelunche in UNA VISTA offerse :
E quel, che'l bello, e'l caro accresce à l'opre,
L'Arte, che tutto fà, nulla si scopre.

Tasso. C. xvi. S. ix.

This, I say, may be the truest taste in gardening, because the simplest : Yet there is a manifest regard to unity in the other method ; which has had it's admirers, as it may have again, and is certainly not without it's *design* and beauty.

But to return to our poet. Thus far he drew from Gothic ideas, and these ideas, I think, would lead him no farther. But, as Spenser knew what belonged to classic composition, he was tempted to tie his subject still closer together by *one* expedient of his own, and by *another* taken from his classic models.

His *own* was to interrupt the proper story of each book, by dispersing it into several ; involving by this means, and as it were intertwisting the several actions together, in order to give something like the appearance of one action to his twelve adventures. And for this conduct, as absurd as it seems, he had some great examples in the Italian poets, tho' I believe, they were led into it by different motives.

The *other* expedient which he borrowed from the classics, was by adopting one superior character, which should be seen throughout. Prince Arthur, who had a separate adventure of his own, was to have his part in each of the other ; and thus several actions were to be embodied by the interest which one principal Hero had in them all. It is even observable, that Spenser gives this adventure of Prince Arthur, in quest of Gloriana, as the proper subject of his poem. And upon this idea the late learned editor of the Faery Queen has attempted, but I think[1] without success, to defend the Unity and simplicity of it's fable. The truth was, the violence of classic prejudices forced the poet to affect this appearance of unity, tho' in contradiction to his gothic system. And, as far as we can judge of the tenour of the whole work from the finished half of it, the adventure of Prince Arthur, whatever the author pretended, and his critic too easily believed, was but an after thought ; and at least with regard to the *historical fable*, which we are now considering, was only one of the expedients by which he would conceal the disorder of his Gothic plan.

And if this was his design, I will venture to say that both his expedients were injudicious. Their purpose was to ally two things, in nature incompatible, the Gothic, and the classic unity ; the effect of which mis-alliance was to discover and expose the nakedness of the Gothic.

I am of opinion then, considering the Faery Queen as an epic or *narrative* poem constructed on Gothic

---

[1] but, I think,

ideas,

ideas, that the Poet had done well to affect no other unity than that of *design*, by which his subject was connected. But his poem is not simply narrative ; it is throughout *Allegorical :* he calls it *a perpetual allegory or dark conceit :* and this character, for reasons I may have occasion to observe hereafter, was even predominant in the Faery Queen. His narration is subservient to his moral, and but serves to colour it. This he tells us himself at setting out.

Fierce wars and faithful loves shall *moralize* my song,

that is, shall serve for a vehicle, or instrument to convey the moral.

Now under this idea, the *Unity* of the Faery Queen is more apparent. His twelve knights are to exemplify as many virtues, out of which one illustrious character is to be composed. And in this view the part of Prince Arthur in each book becomes *essential,* and yet not *principal*; exactly, as the poet has contrived it. They who rest in the literal story, that is, who criticize it on the footing of a narrative poem, have constantly objected to this management. They say, it necessarily breaks the unity of design. Prince Arthur, they affirm, should either have had no part in the other adventures, or he should have had the chief part.[1] He should either have done nothing, or more. And the objection is unanswerable ; at least I know of nothing that can be said to remove it but what I have supposed above might be the purpose of the poet, and which I myself have rejected as insufficient.

But how faulty soever this conduct be in the literal story, it is perfectly right in the *moral :* and that for an obvious reason, tho' his critics seem not to have been aware of it.   His chief hero was not to have the twelve virtues in the *degree* in which the knights had, each of them, their own ; (such a character would be a monster) [1] but he was to have so much of each as was requisite to form his superior character.   Each virtue, in it's perfection, is exemplified in it's own knight : they are all, in a due degree, concenter'd [2] in Prince Arthur.

This was the poet's *moral :* And what way of expressing this moral in the *history*, but by making Prince Arthur appear in each adventure, and in a manner subordinate to it's proper hero ?   Thus, tho' inferior to each in his own specific virtue, he is superior to all by uniting the whole circle of their virtues in himself : And thus he arrives, at length, at the possession of that bright form of *Glory*, whose ravishing beauty, as seen in a dream or vision, had led him out into these miraculous adventures in the land of Faery.

The conclusion is, that, as an *allegorical* poem, the method of the Faery Queen is governed by the justness of the *moral :* As a *narrative* poem, it is conducted

[1] their own (such a character would be a monster ;)
[2] concentrated

on the ideas and usages of *chivalry*. In either view, if taken by itself, the plan is defensible. But from the union of the two designs there arises a perplexity and confusion, which is the proper, and only considerable, defect of this extraordinary poem.

L E T T E R IX.

NO doubt Spenser might have taken one single adventure, of the TWELVE, for the subject of his Poem ; or he might have given the principal part in every adventure to P.[1] Arthur. By this means his fable had been of the classic kind, and it's unity as strict as that of Homer and Virgil.

All this the poet knew very well,[2] but his purpose was not to write a classic poem. He chose to adorn a gothic story ; and, to be consistent throughout, he chose that the *form* of his work shoud[3] be of a piece with his subject.

Did the Poet do right in this ? I cannot tell,[4] but comparing his work with that of another great Poet, who followed the system you seem to recommend, I see no reason to be peremptory in condemning his judgment.

The example of this poet deserves to be considered. It will afford, at least, a fresh confirmation of the point,

I principally insist upon, I mean, *The preeminence of the Gothic manners* [1] *and fictions, as adapted to the ends of poetry, above the classic.*

I observed of the famous Torquato Tasso, that, coming into the world a little of the latest for the success of the pure Gothic manner, he thought fit to *trim* between that and the classic model.

It was lucky for his fame, perhaps, that [2] he did so. For the gothic fables falling every day more and more into contempt, and the learning of the times, throughout all Europe, taking a classic turn, the reputation of his work has been chiefly founded on the strong resemblance it has to the antient epic poems. His fable is conducted in the spirit of the Iliad, and with a strict regard to that unity of *action* which we admire in Homer and Virgil.

But this is not all; we find a studied and close imitation of those poets, in many of the smaller parts, in the minuter incidents, and even in the descriptions, and similies of his poem.

The classic reader was pleased with this deference to the public taste : he saw with delight the favourite beauties of Homer and Virgil reflected in the Italian

[1] I principally insist upon the pre-eminence of the GOTHIC manners

[2] fame that

poet :

poet : and was almost ready to excuse, for the sake of these, his magic tales and faery enchantments.

I said, was *almost ready* ; for the offence given by these to [1] the more fashionable sort of critics was so great, that nothing, I believe, could make full amends, in their judgment, for such extravagancies.

However, by this means the *Gierusalemme Liberata* made it's fortune amongst the French wits, who have constantly cried it up above the *Orlando furioso*, and principally for this reason, that Tasso was more classical in his fable, and more sparing in the wonders of gothic fiction, than his Predecessor.

The Italians have indeed a predilection for their elder bard, whether from their prejudice for antiquity ; [2] their admiration of his language ; the richness of his invention ; the comic air of his style and manner ; or from whatever other reason.

Be this as it will, the French criticism has carried it before the Italian, with the rest of Europe. This dextrous people have found means to lead the taste, as well as set the fashions, of their neighbours : And Ariosto ranks but little higher than the rudest romancer in the opinion of those who take their notions of these things from their writers.

But the same principle, which made them give Tasso
the preference to Ariosto, has led them by degrees to
think very unfavorably of Tasso himself. The mixture
of the gothic manner in his work has not been forgiven.
It has sunk the credit of all the rest ; and some instances
of false taste in the expression of his sentiments, detected,
by their nicer critics, have brought matters to that
pass, that, with their good will, Tasso himself should
now follow the fate of Ariosto.

I will not say, that a little national envy did not
perhaps mix itself with their other reasons for under-
valuing this great poet. They aspired to a sort of
supremacy in Letters ; and finding the Italian language
and its best writers standing in their way, they have
spared no pains to lower the estimation of both.

Whatever their inducements were, they succeeded
but too well in their attempt. Our obsequious and
over modest critics were run down by their authority.
Their taste of Letters, with some worse things, was
brought amongst us at the Restoration. Their language, their manners, nay their very prejudices were
adopted by our Frenchified [1] king and his Royalists.
And the more fashionable wits, of course, set their
fancies, as my Lord Molesworth tells us the people of
Copenhagen in his time did their clocks, by the court-
standard.

[1] polite

Sir

Sir W. Davenant open'd the way to this new sort
of criticism in a very elaborate preface to Gondibert;
and his philosophic friend, Mr. Hobbes, lent his best
assistance towards establishing the credit of it. These
two fine Letters contain, indeed, the substance of
whatever has been since written on the subject.
Succeeding wits and critics did no more than echo
their language. It grew into a sort of cant, with which
Rymer, and the rest of that School, filled their flimsy
essays and rambling prefaces.

Our noble critic himself * condescended to take up
this trite theme : And it is not to be told with what
alacrity and self-complacency he flourishes upon it.
The *Gothic manner*, as he calls it, is the favourite object
of his raillery ; which is never more lively or pointed,
than when it exposes that " bad taste which makes us
" prefer an Ariosto to a Virgil, and a Romance (without
" doubt he meant, of Tasso) to an Iliad." Truly, this
critical sin requires an expiation, which is easily made
by subscribing to his sentence, " That the French
" indeed may boast of legitimate authors of a just
" relish ; but that the Italian are good for nothing
" but to corrupt the taste of those who have had no
" familiarity with the noble antients." [1]

This ingenious nobleman is, himself, one of the
gallant votaries he sometimes makes himself so merry

* Lord Shaftesbury, *Adv. to an Author.*
[1] ancients ƒ   ƒ *Adv. to an Author*, Pt. III. S. ii.

with

with. He is perfectly enamoured of his *noble antients*, and will fight with any man who contends, not that his Lordship's mistress is not fair, but that his own is fair also.

It is certain the French wits benefited by this foible. For pretending, in great modesty, to have formed themselves on the pure taste of his noble ancients, they easily drew his Lordship over to their party : While the Italians more stubbornly pretending to a taste of their own, and chusing to *lye* for themselves, instead of adopting the authorized *lyes* of Greece, were justly exposed to his resentment.

Such was the address of the French writers, and such their triumphs over the poor Italians.

It must be owned, indeed, they had every advantage on their side, in this contest with their masters. The taste and learning of Italy had been long on the decline,[1] and the fine writers under Louis XIV were every day advancing the French language, such as it is, (simple clear, exact, that is, fit for business and conversation ; but for that reason, besides it's total want of numbers, absolutely unsuited to the genius of the greater poetry) towards it's last perfection. The purity of the antient manner became well understood, and it was the pride of their best critics to expose every instance of false taste in the modern writers. The Italian, it is certain, could not stand so severe a scrutiny. But they had

[1] decline

escaped

escaped better, if the most fashionable of the French
poets had not, at the same time, been their best critic.

A lucky word in a verse, which sounds well and every
body gets by heart, goes farther[1] than a volume of just
criticism. In short, the exact, but cold Boileau happened to say something of the *clinquant* of Tasso ; and
the magic of this word, like the report of Astolfo's horn
in Ariosto, overturned at once the solid and well built
reputation of the Italian poetry.

It is not perhaps so amazing [2] that this potent word
should do it's business in France. It [3] put us into
a fright on this side the water. Mr. Addison, who
gave the law in taste here, took it up[4] and sent it about
the kingdom in his polite and popular essays.[5] It
became a sort of watch-word among the critics ; and,
on the sudden, nothing was heard, on all sides, but the
clinquant of Tasso.

After all, these two respectable writers might not
intend the mischief they were doing. The observation
was just, but was extended much farther [6] than they
meant, by their witless followers and admirers. The
effect was, as I said, that the Italian poetry was rejected
in the gross, by virtue of this censure ; tho' the authors
of it had said no more than this, " That their best poet

" had some false thoughts, and dealt, as they supposed,
" too much in incredible fiction."

I leave you to make your own reflexions on this short
history of the Italian poetry. It is not my design to
make it's apology [1] in all respects. However, with
regard to the *first* of these charges, I presume to say [2]
that, as just as it is in the sense in which I persuade
myself it was intended, there are more instances of
natural sentiment [3] and of that divine simplicity we
admire in the antients, even in Guarini's *Pastor Fido*,
than in the best of the French poets.

And as to the *last*,[4] I pretend to shew you, in my
next Letter, that it is no fault at all in the Italian poets.

LETTER X.

CHI non sa che cosa sia Italia ?—If this question
could ever be reasonably asked on any occasion, it
must surely be when the wit and poetry of that
people were under consideration. The enchanting sweet-
ness of their tongue, the richness of their invention, the
fire and elevation of their genius, the splendor of their
expression on great subjects, and the native simplicity
of their sentiments, on affecting ones ; All these are
such manifest advantages on the side of the Italian

---

[1] be its apologist   [2] say,   [3] sentiment,
[4] *last* charge,   [5] splendour

poets,

poets, as should seem to command our highest admiration of their great and capital works.

Yet a different language has been held by our finer critics. And in particular you hear it commonly said of the tales of Faery, which they first and principally adorned, " That they are unnatural [1] and absurd; " that they surpass all bounds not of truth only, but of " probability; and look more like the dreams of " children, than the manly inventions of poets."

All this, and more, has been said; and if truely [2] said, who would not lament

L'arte del poëtar troppo infelice ?

For they are not the cold fancies of plebeian poets, but the golden dreams of Ariosto, the celestial visions of Tasso, that are thus derided.[3]

The only criticism, indeed that is worth regarding is, the philosophical.[4] But there is a sort which looks like philosophy, and is not. May not that be the case here ?

This criticism, whatever name it deserves, supposes

reasonable. They think it enough, if they can but bring you to *imagine* the possibility of them.

And how small a matter will serve for this ? A legend, a tale, a tradition, a rumour, a superstition ; in short, any thing is enough to be the basis of their air-form'd *visions*. Does any capable reader trouble himself about the truth, or even the credibility of their fancies ? Alas, no ; he is best pleased when he is made to conceive (he minds not by what magic) the existence of such things as his reason tells him did not, and were never likely to, exist.

But here, to prevent mistakes, an explanation will be necessary. We must distinguish between the *popular belief*, and *that of the Reader*. The fictions of poetry do, in some degree at least, require the *first* ; (They[1] would, otherwise, deservedly pass for *dreams* indeed) : But when the poet has this advantage on his side, and his fancies have, or may be supposed to have, a countenance from the current superstitions of the age, in which he writes, he dispenses with the *last*, and gives his Reader leave to be as sceptical and as incredulous, as he pleases.

An eminent French critic diverts himself with imagining " what a person, who comes fresh from " reading Mr. Addison and Mr. Lock,[2] would be apt to " think of Tasso's Enchantment *."

[1] *first* (they   [2] Locke
* Voltaire, *Essai sur la Poësie Epique*, Ch. vii.

The

The English reader will, perhaps, smile at seeing these two writers so coupled together : And, with the critic's leave, we will put Mr. Lock[1] out of the question. But if he be desirous to know what a reader of Mr. Addison would pronounce in the case, I can undertake to give him satisfaction.

Speaking of what Mr. Dryden calls, *the Faery way of writing,* " Men of cold fancies and philosophical " dispositions, says he, object to this kind of poetry, " that it has not probability enough to affect the " imagination. But . . . many are prepossest with such " false opinions, as dispose them to *believe* these par- " ticular delusions : At least, we have all *hear'd* so " many pleasing relations in favour of them, that we " do not care for seeing thro' the *falshood*,[2] and willingly " give ourselves up to so agreable[3] an imposture." [*Spect.* V. vi.][4]

Apply, now, this sage judgment of Mr. Addison to *Tasso's Enchantments*,[2] and you see that a *falshood*[5] *convict* is not to be pleaded against a *supposed belief,* or even the *slightest hear-say.*

So little account does this wicked poetry make of philosophical or historical truth : All she allows us to look for, is *poetical truth* ; a very slender thing indeed,

frenzy,[1] can but just lay hold of.\ To speak in the philosophic language of Mr. Hobbes, It is something much *beyond the actual bounds, and only within the conceived possibility, of*[2] *nature.*

\ But the source of bad criticism, as universally of bad philosophy, is the abuse of terms. A poet, they say, must follow *Nature*; and by Nature we are to suppose can only be meant the known and experienced course of affairs in this world. Whereas the poet has a world of his own, where experience has less to do, than consistent imagination.

He has, besides, a supernatural world to range in. He has Gods, and Faeries, and Witches at his command: and,

> — — — — O! who can tell
> The hidden *pow'r* of herbes, and might of magic spell?
> Spenser. B. i.[3] C. 2.

Thus[4] in the poet's world, all is marvellous and extraordinary; yet not *unnatural* in one sense, as it agrees to the conceptions that are readily entertained of these magical and wonder-working Natures.

This trite maxim of *following Nature* is further mistaken[5] in applying it indiscriminately to all sorts of poetry.

---

[1] *fine frenzy,*
[3] B. v. (But B. i. is correct. Ed.)
[5] mistaken,
[2] *possibility of*
[4] Thus,

In

In those species which have men and manners professedly for their theme, a strict conformity with human nature is reasonably demanded. ✓

Non hic Centauros, non Gorgonas, Harpyiasque
Invenies : hominem pagina nostra sapit

is a proper motto to a book of Epigrams,[1] but would make a poor figure at the head of an epic poem.

Still further, in[2] those species that address themselves to the heart[3] and would obtain their end, not thro' the Imagination, but thro' the *Passions*, there the liberty of transgressing nature, I mean the real powers and properties of human nature, is infinitely restrained ; and *poetical* truth is, under these circumstances, almost as severe a thing as *historical*.

The reason is, we must first *believe*, before we can be *affected*.

But the case is different with the more sublime and creative poetry. This species, addressing itself solely

This difference, you will say, is obvious enough. How came it then to be overlooked ? From another mistake, in extending a particular precept of the drama into a general maxim.

. The *incredulus odi* of Horace ran in the heads of these critics, tho' his own words confine the observation singly to the stage.

> Segnius irritant animos demissa per aurem
> Quam quæ sunt oculis subjecta fidelibus, et quæ
> Ipse sibi tradit Spectator——

That, which passes in *representation* and challenges, as it were, the scrutiny of the eye, must be truth itself, or something very nearly approaching to it. But what passes in *narration*, even on the stage, is admitted without much difficulty—

> multaque tolles
> Ex oculis, quæ mox narret facundia præsens.[1]

In the epic narration, which may be called *absens facundia*, the reason of the thing shews this indulgence to be still greater. It appeals neither to the *eye* nor the *ear*, but simply to the *imagination*, and so allows the poet a liberty of multiplying and enlarging his impostures at pleasure, in proportion to the easiness and comprehension of that faculty.[2]

[1] presens
[2] faculty [1]. (For note in 1788 edition see Appendix J.)

These

These general reflexions hardly require an application to the present subject. The tales of faery are exploded, as fantastic and incredible. They would merit this contempt, if presented on the stage ; I mean, if they were given as the proper subject of dramatic imitation, and the interest of the poet's plot were to be wrought out of the adventures of these marvellous persons. But the epic muse runs no risque in giving way to such fanciful exhibitions.

You may call them, as one does, " extraordinary " dreams, such as excellent poets and painters, by " being over studious, may have in the beginning of " fevers [b]."

The epic poet would acknowledge the charge, and even value himself upon it. He would say, " I leave to the sage dramatist the merit of being always broad awake, and always in his senses : The *divine dream* [c], and delirious fancy, are among the noblest of my prerogatives."

But the injustice done the Italian poets does not stop here. The cry is, " Magic and enchantments " are senseless things. Therefore the Italian poets are " not worth the reading." As if, because the superstitions of Homer and Virgil are no longer believed, their

Yes, you will say, their fine pictures of life and manners—

And may not I say the same, in behalf of Ariosto and Tasso? For it is not true that all is *unnatural* and monstrous in their poems, because of this mixture of the wonderful. Admit, for example, Armida's marvellous conveyance to the happy Island, and all the rest of the love-story is as natural, that is, as suitable to our common notions of that passion, as any thing in Virgil or (if you will) Voltaire.

Thus you see[1] the apology of the Italian poets is easily made on every supposition. But I stick to my point and maintain that the faery tales of Tasso do him more honour than what are called the more natural, that is, the classical parts of his poem. His imitations of the antients have indeed their merit; for he was a genius in every thing. But they are faint and cold[2] and almost insipid, when compared with his original[3] fictions. We make a shift to run over the passages he has copied from Virgil. We are all on fire amidst the magical feats of Ismen, and the enchantments of Armida.

> Magnanima mensogna, hor quando è il vero
> Si bello, che si possa à te preporre?

I speak at least for myself; and must freely own,

---

[1] Thus, you see,   [2] cold,   [3] *Gothic*

if it were not for these *Lyes* of Gothic invention, I should scarcely be disposed to give the *Gierusalemme Liberata* a second reading.

I readily agree to the lively observation, "That "impenetrable armour, inchanted castles, invulnerable "bodies, iron men, flying horses, and other such things, "are easily feigned by them that dare [*d*]." But, with the observer's leave, not so feigned as we find them in the Italian poets, unless the writer have another quality, besides that of courage.

One thing is true, that the success of these fictions will not be great, when they have no longer any footing in the popular belief : And the reason is, that readers do not usually do,[1] as they ought, put themselves in the circumstances of the poet, or rather of those, of whom the poet writes. But this only shews, that some ages are not so fit to write epic poems in, as others ; not, that they should be otherwise written.

It is also true, that writers do not succeed so well in painting what they have heard, as what they believe[2] themselves, or at least observe in others a facility of believing. And on this account I would advise no modern poet to revive these faery tales in an epic poem. But still this is nothing to the case in hand, where we are

The pagan Gods, and Gothic Faeries were equally out of credit, when Milton wrote. He did well therefore to supply their room with angels and devils. If these too should wear out of the popular creed (and they seem in a hopeful way, from the liberty some late critics have taken with them) I know not what other expedients the epic poet might have recourse to ; but this I know, the pomp of verse, the energy of description, and even the finest moral paintings would stand him in no stead. Without *admiration* (which cannot be effected but by the marvellous of celestial intervention, I mean, the agency of superior natures really existing, or by the illusion of the fancy taken to be so) no epic poem can be long-lived.

I am not afraid to instance in the Henriade itself ; which, notwithstanding the elegance of the composition, will in a short time be no more read than the Gondibert of Sir W. Davenant, and for the same reason.

Critics may talk what they will of *Truth and Nature*, and abuse the Italian poets,[1] as they will, for transgressing both in their incredible fictions. But believe it, my friend, these fictions with which they have studied to delude the world, are of that kind of creditable deceits, of which a wise antient pronounces with assurance, " *That they, who deceive, are honester than* " *they who do not deceive ; and they, who are deceived,* " *wiser than they who are not deceived.*"

_____
[1] poets

L E T-

BUT you are weary of hearing so much of these exploded fancies ; and are ready to ask, if there be any truth in this representation, " Whence it has come " to pass, that the classical manners are still admired " and imitated by the poets, when the Gothic have " long since fallen into disuse ?

The answer to this question will furnish all that is now wanting to a proper discussion of the present subject.

ONE great reason of this difference certainly was, That the ablest writers of Greece ennobled the system of heroic manners, while it was fresh and flourishing ; and their works, being master-pieces of composition, so fixed the credit of it in the opinion of the world, that no revolutions of time and taste could afterwards shake it.

Whereas the Gothic having been disgraced in their infancy by bad writers, and a new set of manners springing up before there were any better to do them justice, they could never be brought into vogue by the attempts of later poets ; who [1] in spite of prejudice, and for the genuine charm of these highly poetical

But, FURTHER, the Gothic system was not only forced to wait long for real genius to do it honour; real genius was even very early employed against it.

There were two causes of this mishap. The old romancers had even outraged the truth in their extravagant pictures of chivalry : And Chivalry itself, such as it once had been, was greatly abated.

So that men of sense were doubly disgusted to find a representation of things *unlike* to what they observed in real life, and *beyond* what it was ever possible should have existed. However, with these disadvantages [1] there was still so much of the old spirit left, and the fascination of these wondrous tales was so prevalent, that a more than common degree of sagacity and good sense was required to penetrate the illusion.

It was one of this character, I suppose, that put the famous question to Ariosto, which has been so often repeated that I shall spare you the disgust of hearing it. Yet long before his time an immortal genius of our own (so superior is the sense of some men to the age they live in) saw as far into this matter, as Ariosto's examiner. This sagacious person [2] was Dan Chaucer ; who in a reign, that almost realized the wonders of romantic chivalry, not only discerned the absurdity of the old

---

[1] disadvantages,

[2] You will, perhaps, be as much surprised as I was (when, many years ago, the observation was, first, made to me) to understand, that this sagacious person

romances,

romances, but has even ridiculed them with incomparable spirit.

His Rime of Sir Topaz in the Canterbury tales,[1] is a manifest banter on these books, and may be considered as a sort of prelude to the adventures of Don Quixot.[2] I call it *a manifest banter*: For we are to observe that this was Chaucer's own tale, and that, when in the progress of it the good sense of the Host is made to break in upon him, and interrupt him, Chaucer approves his disgust and, changing his note, tells the simple instructive tale of Meliboeus, *a moral tale virtuous*, as he chuses to characterize[3] it; to shew, what sort of fictions were most expressive of real life, and most proper to be put into the hands of the people.[4]

One might further observe that the Rime of Sir Topaz itself is so managed as with infinite humour to expose the leading impertinences of books of chivalry, and their impertinencies only; as may be seen by the different conduct of this tale, from that of Cambuscan, which Spenser and Milton were so pleased with, and which with great propriety is put into the mouth of the Squire.

---

[1] " His Rime of Sir Topaz in the *Canterbury* Tales, (said the curious observer, on whose authority I am now building)
[2] Quixote   [3] terms it

But I must not anticipate the observations which you will take a pleasure to make for yourself on these two fine parts of the Canterbury tales. Enough is said to illustrate the point, I am now upon, " That these " phantoms of chivalry had the misfortune to be " laughed out of countenance by men of sense, before " the substance of it had been fairly and truly repre- " sented by any capable writer."

STILL, the principal reason of all, no doubt, was, That the Gothic manners of Chivalry, as springing [1] out of the feudal system, were as singular, as that system itself: So that, when that political constitution vanished out of Europe, the manners, that belonged to it, were no longer seen or understood. There was no example of any such manners remaining on the face of the Earth: And as they never did subsist but once, and are never likely to subsist again, people would be led of course to think and speak of them, as romantic, and unnatural. The consequence of which was a total contempt and rejection of them; while the classic manners, as arising out of the customary and usual situations of humanity, would have many archetypes, and appear natural even to those who saw nothing similar to them actually subsisting before their eyes.

[1] cause of all, which brought disgrace on the *Gothic* manners of Chivalry, no doubt, was, That these manners, which sprang out

Thus,

Thus, tho' the manners of Homer are perhaps as different from our's, as those of Chivalry itself, yet as we know that such manners always belong to rude and simple ages, such as Homer paints ; and actually subsist at this day in countries that are under the like circumstances of barbarity, we readily agree to call them *natural*, and even take a fond pleasure in the survey of them.

Your question then is easily answered, without any obligation upon me to give up the Gothic manners as visionary and fantastic. And the reason appears, why the *Faery Queen*, one of the noblest productions of modern poetry, is fallen into so general a neglect, that all the zeal of it's commentators is esteemed officious and impertinent, and will never restore it to those honours which it has, once for all, irrecoverably lost.

In effect, what way of persuading the generality of readers that the romantic manners are to be accounted *natural*, when not one in ten-thousand knows enough of the barbarous ages, in which they arose, to believe they ever really existed ?

must, for ought [1] I can see, be left to the admiration of a few lettered and curious men : While the many are sworn together to give no quarter to the *marvellous*, or, which may seem still harder, to the *moral* of his song.

However this great revolution in modern taste was brought about by degrees; and the steps, that led to it, may be worth the tracing in a distinct Letter.

LETTER XII.

THE wonders of Chivalry were still in the memory of men, were still existing, in some measure, in real life, when Chaucer undertook to expose the barbarous relaters of them.

This ridicule, we may suppose, hastened the fall both of Chivalry and Romance. At least from that time the spirit of both declined very fast, and at length fell into such discredit, that when now Spenser arose, and with a genius singularly fitted to immortalize the land of faery, he met with every difficulty and disadvantage to obstruct his design.

The age would no longer bear the naked letter of these amusing stories; and the poet was so sensible of the misfortune, that we find him apologizing for it on a hundred occasions.

[1] aught

But

But apologies, in such circumstances, rarely do any good. Perhaps, they only served to betray the weakness of the poet's cause, and to confirm the prejudices of his reader.

However, he did more than this. He gave an air of mystery to his subject, and pretended that his stories of knights and giants were but the cover to abundance of profound wisdom.

In short, to keep off the eyes of the prophane from prying too nearly into his subject, he threw about it the mist of allegory: he moralized his song: and the virtues and vices lay hid under his warriours[1] and enchanters. A contrivance which he had learned indeed from his Italian masters: For Tasso had condescended to allegorize his own work; and the commentators of Ariosto had even converted the extravagances of the Orlando Furioso, into moral lessons.

And this, it must be owned, was a sober attempt in comparison of some projects that were made about the same time to serve the cause of the old, and now expiring Romances. For it is to be observed, that the idolizers of these[2] romances did by them, what the votaries of Homer had done by him. As the times improved and would less bear his strange tales, they

mysteries of *natural science*. And as this last contrivance was principally designed to cover the monstrous stories of the *pagan Gods*, so it served the lovers of Romance to palliate the no less monstrous stories of *magic and enchantments*.[1]

The editor, or translator of the 24th book of *Amadis de Gaule*, printed at Lyons in 1577, has a preface explaining the whole secret, which concludes with these words, " Voyla, Lecteur, le FRUIT, qui se peut recueiller du sens mystique des Romans antiques par les ESPRITS ESLEUS, le commun peuple soy contentant de la simple FLEUR DE LA LECTURE LITERALE.

But to return to Spenser ; who, as we have seen, had no better way to take in his distress, than to hide his faery fancies under the mystic cover of moral allegory. The only favourable circumstance that attended him (and this no doubt encouraged, if it did not produce[2] his untimely project) was, that he was somewhat befriended in these fictions, even when interpreted according to the Letter, by the romantic Spirit of his age ; much countenanced, and for a time brought into fresh credit, by the romantic Elizabeth. Her inclination for the fancies of Chivalry is well known ; and obsequious wits and courtiers would not be wanting to feed and flatter it. In short, tilts and tournaments were in vogue : The Arcadia, and the Faery Queen were written.

[1] *magic enchantments.*   [2] produce,

With

With these helps the new Spirit of Chivalry made a shift to support itself for a time, when reason was but dawning, as we may say, and just about to gain the ascendant over the portentous spectres of the imagination. It's growing splendour, in the end, put them all to flight, and allowed them no quarter even amongst the poets. So that Milton, as fond as we have seen he was of the Gothic fictions, durst only admit them on the bye, and in the way of simile and illustration only.

And this, no doubt, was the main reason of his relinquishing his long-projected design of Prince Arthur, at last, for that of the Paradise Lost; where, instead of Giants and Magicians, he had Angels and Devils to supply him with the *marvellous*, with greater probability. Yet, tho' he dropped the tales, he still kept to the allegories of Spenser. And even this liberty was thought too much, as appears from the censure passed on his *Sin and Death* by the severer critics.

Thus at length the magic of the old romances was perfectly dissolved. They began with reflecting an image indeed of the feudal manners, but an image magnified and distorted by unskilful designers. Com-

step was to have recourse to *allegories*. Under this disguise they walked the world a while ; the excellence of the moral and the ingenuity of the contrivance making some amends, and being accepted as a sort of apology, for the absurdity of the literal story.

Under this form the tales of faery kept their ground, and even made their fortune at court ; where they became, for two or three reigns, the ordinary entertainment of our princes. But reason, in the end, (assisted however by party, and religious prejudices) [1] drove them off the scene, and would endure these *lying wonders*, neither in their own proper shape, nor as masked in figures.

Henceforth, the taste of wit and poetry took a new turn : And *fancy*, that had [2] wantoned it so long in the world of fiction, was now constrained, against her will, to ally herself with strict truth, if she would gain admittance into reasonable company. [3]

What we have gotten by this revolution, you will say, is a great deal of good sense. What we have lost, is a world of fine fabling ; the illusion of which is so grateful to the *charmed Spirit* ; that, in spite of philosophy and fashion, *Faery* Spenser still ranks

[1] prejudices),   [2] And the *Muse*, who had
[3] against her will,
    " To stoop with disenchanted wings to truth,"
as Sir JOHN DENHAM somewhere expresses her present enforced state, not unhappily.

highest

highest among the Poets ; I mean with all those who are either come of that house, or have any kindness for it.

Earth-born critics, my friend, may blaspheme,[1]

> " But all the GODS are ravish'd with delight
> "Of his celestial Song, and music's wondrous might."

[1] blaspheme :

The E N D.

A P P E N D I X A.[1]

AND yet (so slippery is the ground, on which we system-makers stand) from what I observed of the spirit, with which the Crusades were carried on, a hint may be taken, which threatens to overturn my whole system.

It is, ' That, whereas I derive the Crusades from the spirit of Chivalry, the circumstances attending the progress of the Crusades, and even as pointed out by myself, seem to favour the opposite opinion of Chivalry's taking its rise from that enterprize.'

For thus the argument is drawn out by a learned person,[a] to whom I communicated the substance of my last Letter.

"On the crumbling of the Western empire into small states, with regular subordinations of vassals and their chiefs, who looked up to a common sovereign, it was soon found that those chiefs had it in their power to make themselves very formidable to their masters; and, just in that crisis of European manners and empire, the *Saracens* having expelled Christianity from the East, the Western Princes seized the opportunity, and with great craft turned the warlike genius of their feudatories, which would otherwise have preyed

[1] See Letter IV, p. 93.
[a] The late right honourable Charles Yorke; who to all the learning of his own profession had joined an exact taste, and very extensive knowledge, of polite literature. What follows is an extract from a long letter which this excellent person did me the honour to write to me on the subject of these letters, when he had read them in the first edition.

upon

upon themselves, into the spirit of Crusades against the common enemy.

But when, now, the ardour of the Crusades was abated in some sort, though not extinguished, the *Gothic* princes and their families had settled into established monarchies. Then it was, that the restless spirit of their vassals, having little employment abroad, and being restrained in a good degree from exerting itself with success in domestic quarrels, broke out in all the extravagances of Knight-Errantry.

Military fame, acquired in the Holy land, had entitled the adventurers to the *insignia* of arms, the source of Heraldry; and inspired them with the love of war and the passion of enterprize. Their late expeditions had given them a turn for roving in quest of adventures; and their religious zeal had infused high notions of piety, justice, and chastity.

The scene of action being now more confined, they turned themselves, from *the world's debate*, to private and personal animosities. Chivalry was employed in rescuing humble and faithful vassals, from the oppression of petty lords; their women, from savage lust; and the hoary heads of hermits (a species of Eastern monks, much reverenced in the Holy land), from rapine and outrage.

In the mean time the courts of the feudal sovereigns grew magnificent and polite; and, as the military constitution still subsisted, military merit was to be upheld; but, wanting its old objects, it naturally softened into the fictitious images and courtly exercises of war in *justs and tournaments*: where

holy Sepulchre ; and thus the courtesy of elegant love, but of a wild and fanatic species, as being engrafted on spiritual enthusiasm, came to mix itself with the other characters of the Knights-errant.''

In this way, you see, all the characteristics of Chivalry, which I had derived from the essential properties of the feudal government, are made to result from the spirit of Crusades, which with me was only an accidental effect of it : and this deduction may be thought to agree best with the representation of the old Romancers.

This hypothesis, so plausible in itself, is very ingeniously supported. Yet I have something to object to it ; or rather, which flatters me more, I think I can turn it to the advantage of my own system.

For what if I allow (as indeed I needs must) that *Chivalry,* such as we have it represented in books of Romance, so much posterior to the date of that military institution, took its colour and character from the impressions made on the minds of men by the spirit of Crusading into the Holy land ? Still it may be true, that Chivalry itself had properly another and an earlier origin. And I must think it certainly *had,* if for no other, yet for this reason : that, unless the seeds of that spirit, which appeared in the Crusades, had been plentifully sown and indeed grown up into some maturity in the feudal times preceding that event, I see not how it could have been possible for the Western princes to give that politic diversion to their turbulent vassals, which the new hypothesis supposes.

In

In short, there are TWO DISTINCT PERIODS to be carefully observed, in a deduction of the rise and progress of Chivalry.

The FIRST is that in which the empire was overturned, and the feudal governments were every where introduced on its ruins, by the Northern nations. In this æra, that new policy settled itself in the West, and operated so powerfully as to lay the first foundations, and to furnish the remote causes, of what we know by the name of Chivalry.

The OTHER period is, when these causes had taken a fuller effect, and shewed themselves in that signal enterprize of the Crusades ; which not only concurred with the spirit of Chivalry, already pullulating in the minds of men, but brought a prodigious encrease, and gave a singular force and vigour to all its operations. In this æra, Chivalry took deep root, and at the same time shot up to its full height and size. So that now it was in the state of Virgil's Tree—

—Quae quantum vertice ad auras
Æthereas, tantum radice in Tartara tendit.
Ergo non hiemes illam, non flabra, neque imbres
Convellunt : immota manet, multosque per annos
Multa virûm volvens durando sæcula vincit.

From this last period, the Romancers, whether in prose or verse, derive all their ideas of Chivalry. It was *natural* for them to do so ; for they were best acquainted with that

and so distinctly marked as fitted them for the use of description.

But that the former period, notwithstanding, really gave birth to this institution may be gathered, not only from the reason of the thing, but from the surer information of authentic history. For there are traces of Chivalry, in its most peculiar and characteristic forms, to be found in the age preceding the Crusades ; and even justs and tournaments, the *image* of serious Knight-errantry, were certainly of earlier date than that event, as I had before occasion to observe to you.

Though I think, then, my notion *of the rise of Chivalry* stands unimpaired, or rather is somewhat illustrated and confirmed, by what the excellent person has opposed to it, yet I could not hold it fair to conceal so specious and well-supported an objection from you. You are too generous to take advantage of the arms I put into your hands ; and are, besides, so far from any thoughts of combating my system itself, that your concern, it seems, is only to know, where I learned the several particulars, on which I have formed it.

APPENDIX B.[1]

EVEN PLUTARCH's life of THESEUS reads, throughout, like a modern Romance : and Sir ARTHEGAL himself is hardly his fellow, for righting wrongs and redressing grievances. So that EURIPIDES might well make him say of himself, *that he had chosen the profession and calling of a Knight-errant* : for this

---

[1] See Letter IV, p. 99.

is

is the sense, and almost the literal construction, of the following verses :

$$^*Eθος \ τόδ' \ εἰς \ "Ελληνας \ ἐξελεξάμην$$
$$'Αεὶ \ ΚΟΛΑΣΤΗΣ \ ΤΩΝ \ ΚΑΚΩΝ \ καθεςάναι.$$

'Ικέτιδες, ver 340.

Accordingly, THESEUS is a favourite Hero (witness the
Knight's Tale in CHAUCER) even with the Romance-writers.

APPENDIX C.[1]

. . . so great that the observation of it did not escape the
old Romancers themselves, *with whom,* as an ingenious critic
observes, *the siege of* THEBES *and* TROJAN *war were favourite
stories; the characters and incidents of which they were mixing
perpetually with their Romances* [c]. And to this persuasion
and practice of the Romance-writers CERVANTES plainly
alludes, when he makes Don QUIXOTE say——*If the stories of
Chivalry be lies, so must it also be, that there ever was a* HECTOR,
or an ACHILLES, *or a* TROJAN WAR [d]—a sly stroke of satire,
by which this mortal foe of Chivalry would, I suppose,
insinuate that the *Grecian* Romances were just as extravagant
and as little credible, as the *Gothic.* Or, whatever his purpose
might be, the resemblance between them, you see, is confessed, and hath now been shewn in so many instances that
there will hardly be any doubt of it.

[c] Mr. WARTON's Observations on SPENSER, vol. i. p. 175.
[d] Don QUIXOTE, b. iv. c. 22.

APPENDIX D.[1]

Iғ you still insist that I carry this matter too far, and that, in fact, the introduction of the female succession into fiefs was too late to justify me in accounting for the rise of feudal gallantry from that circumstance ; you will only teach me to frame my answer in a more accurate manner.

Fɪʀsᴛ then, I shall confess that the way to avoid all confusion on this subject would be, to distinguish carefully between the state of things in the *early* feudal times, and that in the *later*, when the genius of the feudal law was much changed and corrupted ; and that, whoever would go to the bottom of this affair, should keep a constant eye on this reasonable distinction.

Bᴜᴛ then, *secondly*, I may observe, that this distinction is the less necessary to be attended to in the present case, because the law of female succession, whenever it was introduced, had certainly taken place long before the Romancers wrote, from whom we derive all our ideas of the feudal gallantry. So that, if you take their word for the gallantry of those times, you may very consistently, if you please, accept my account of it. For it is but supposing that the feudal gallantry, such as they paint it, was the offspring of that privilege, such as they saw the ladies then possess, of feudal succession. And the connexion between these two things is so close and so natural, that we cannot be much mistaken in deducing the one from the other.

[1] See Letter V, p. 106.

A P-

APPENDIX E.[1]

IT is true, as to the charge of *domestic licence*, so exactly does the parallel run between old *Greece* and old *England*, I find one exception to it, in each country : and that *one*, a Romance-critic would shew himself very uncourteous, if he did not take a pleasure to celebrate. GUY, the renowned earl of *Warwick*, old stories say, returned from the holy wars to his lady in the disguise of a pilgrim or beggar, as ULYSSES did to PENELOPE. What the suspicions were of the Knight and the Hero, the contrivance itself but too plainly declares. But their fears were groundless in both cases. Only the Knight seems to have had the advantage of the Prince of ITHACA : for, instead of rioting suitors to drive out of his castle, he had only to contemplate his good lady in the peaceful and pious office of *distributing daily alms to* XIII *poor men.*

No conclusion, however, is to be drawn from a single instance ; and, in general, it is said, the adventurers into the Holy Land could no more depend on the fidelity of their spouses, than of their vassals.

APPENDIX F.[2]

YOU will tell me, perhaps, that these fancies, as terrible as they were, are but of a piece with those of Pagan superstition ; and that nothing can exceed what the classic writers have related or feigned of its magic and necromantic horrors.

let me confess to you that many of the antient poets have occasionally adorned this theme. If, among twenty others, I select only the names of OVID, SENECA, and LUCAN, it is, because these writers, by the character of their genius, were best qualified for the task, and have, besides, exerted their whole strength upon it. LUCAN, especially, has drawn out all the pomp of his eloquence in celebrating those THESSALIAN CHARMS,

> ficti quas nulla licentia monstri
> Transierat, quarum, quicquid non creditur, ars est.

YET STILL I pretend to shew you that all his prodigies, fall short of the *Gothic :* and you will come the less reluctantly into my sentiments, if you reflect, "THAT the thick and troubled stream of superstition, which flowed so plentifully in the classic ages, has been constantly deepening and darkening by the confluence of those supplies, which ignorance and corrupted religion have poured in upon it."

FIRST, you will call to mind that all the gloomy visions of dæmons and spirits, which sprung out of the Alexandrian or Platonic philosophy, were in the later ages of Paganism engrafted on the old stock of classic superstition. These portentous dreams, *new hatched to the woful time,* as SHAKE-SPEAR speaks, enabled APULEIUS to outdo LUCAN himself, in some of his magic scenes and exhibitions.

NEXT, you will observe that a fresh and exhaustless swarm of the direst superstitions took their birth in the frozen regions of the north, and were naturally enough conceived in the imaginations of a people involved in tenfold darkness ; I mean, in the thickest shades of ignorance, as well as in the gloom of their comfortless woods and forests. I call these the *direst superstitions ;* for though the south and east may

have

have produced some that shew more wild and fantastic, yet those of the north have ever been of a more sombrous and horrid aspect, agreeably to the singular circumstances and situation of that savage and benighted people.

THESE dismal fancies, which the barbarians carried out with them in their migrations into the north-west, took the readier and the faster hold of men's minds, from the kindred darkness into which the western world was then fallen, and from the desolation (so apt to engender all fearful conceits and apprehensions) which every where attended the incursions of those ravagers.

LASTLY, before the Romancers applied themselves to dress up these dreadful stories, Christian superstition had grown to its height, and had transferred on the magic system all its additional and supernumerary horrors.

TAKING, now, the whole together, you will clearly see what we are to conclude of the *Gothic* system of prodigy and enchantment; which was not so properly a single system, as the aggregate,

> —of all that nature breeds
> Perverse; all monstrous, all prodigious things,
> Which fables yet had feign'd or fear conceiv'd.

For, to the frightful forms of antient necromancy (which easily travelled down to us, when the fairer offspring of pagan invention lost its way, or was swallowed up in the general darkness of the barbarous ages) were now joined the hideous phantasms which had terrified the northern nations; and, to complete the horrid groupe, with these were incorporated the still more tremendous spectres of Christian superstition.

IN

In this state of things, as I said, the Romancers went to work; and with these multiplied images of terror on their minds, you will conclude, without being at the pains to form particular comparisons, that they must manage ill indeed, not to surpass, in this walk of magical incantation, the original classic fablers.

But, if you require a comparison, I can tell you where it is to be made, with much ease, and to great advantage: I mean, in Shakespear's *Macbeth*, where you will find (as his best critic observes) "the *Danish* or *Northern*, intermixed with "the *Greek* and *Roman* enchantments; and all these worked "up together with a sufficient quantity of our own country "superstitions. So that Shakespear's *Witch-Scenes* (as the "same writer adds) are like the *charms* they prepare in one of "them: where the ingredients are gathered from every thing "shocking in the *natural* world; as here, from every thing "absurd in the *moral*."

Or, if you suspect this instance, as deriving somewhat of its force and plausibility from the *magic* hand of this critic, you may turn to another in a great poet of that time; who has been at the pains to make the comparison himself, and whose word, as he gives it in honest prose, may surely be taken.

In a work of B. Jonson, which he calls The Masque of Queens, there are some Witch scenes; written with singular care, and in emulation, as it may seem, of Shakespear's; but certainly with the view (for so he tells us himself) *of reconciling the practice of antiquity to the neoteric, and making it familiar with our popular witchcraft.*

This

THIS Masque is accompanied with notes of the learned author, who had rifled all the stores of antient and modern *Dæmonomagy*, to furnish out his entertainment; and who takes care to inform us, under each head, whence he had fetched the ingredients, out of which it is compounded.

IN this elaborate work of JONSON you have, then, an easy opportunity of comparing the antient, with the modern magic. And though, as he was an idolater of the antients, you will expect him to draw freely from that source, yet from the large use he makes, too, of his other more recent authorities, you will perceive that some of the darkest shades of his picture are owing to hints and circumstances which he had catched, and could only catch, from the *Gothic* enchantments. Even such of these circumstances, as, taken by themselves, seem of less moment, should not be overlooked, since (as the poet well observes of them) *though they be but minutes in ceremony, yet they make the act more dark and full of horror.*

THUS MUCH, then, may serve for a cast of SHAKESPEAR's and JONSON's magic: abundantly sufficient, I must think, to convince you of the superiority of the *Gothic* charms and incantations, to the classic.

APPENDIX G.[1]

HE should either have done nothing, or more. This objection I find insisted upon by SPENSER's best critic [d]; and, I think, the objection is unanswerable: at least, I know

[d] Mr. WARTON, *Obs. on the F. Q.* p. 7. vol. i. *Lond.* 1762.

[1] See Letter VIII, p. 125.

of nothing that can be said to remove it, but what I have supposed above might be the purpose of the poet, and which I myself have rejected as insufficient.

APPENDIX H.[1]

BUT now, as to the *extravagance* of these fictions, it is frequently, I believe, much less than these laughers apprehend.

To give an instance or two, of this sort.

ONE of the strangest circumstances in those books, is that of the *women-warriors*, with which they all abound. BUTLER, in his *Hudibras*, who saw it only in the light of a poetical invention, ridicules it, as a most unnatural idea, with great spirit. Yet in this representation, they did but copy from the manners of the times. ANNA COMNENA tells us, in the life of her father, that the wife of ROBERT the *Norman* fought side by side with her husband, in his battles ; that she would rally the flying soldiers, and lead them back to the charge : and NICETAS observes, that, in the time of MANUEL COMNENA, there were in one Crusade many women, armed like men, on horseback.

What think you now of TASSO's *Clarinda*, whose prodigies of valour I dare say you have often laughed at ? Or, rather, what think you of that constant pair,

> " GILDIPPE et ODOARDO amanti e sposi,
> " In valor d'arme, e in lealtà famosi ? "
>
> C. III. s. 40.

[1] See Letter X, p. 135.

AGAIN :

AGAIN : what can be more absurd and incredible, it is often said, than the vast armies we read of in Romance ? a circumstance, to which MILTON scruples not to allude in those lines of his *Paradise Regained*—

> Such forces met not, nor so wide a camp,
> When AGRICAN with all his northern powers
> Besieg'd *Albracca*, as Romances tell,
> The city' of GALLAPHRONE, from thence to win
> The fairest of her sex, ANGELICA.   B. III. ver. 337.

THE classical reader is much scandalized on these occasions, and never fails to cry out on the impudence of these lying fablers. Yet if he did but reflect on the prodigious swarms which *Europe* sent out in the Crusades, and that the transactions of those days furnished the Romance-writers with their ideas and images, he would see that the marvellous in such stories was modest enough, and did not very much exceed the strict bounds of historical representation.

THE first army, for instance, that marched for the Holy Land, even after all the losses it had sustained by the way, amounted, we are told, when it came to be mustered in the plains of *Asia*, to no less than seven hundred thousand fighting men : a number, which would almost have satisfied the Romancer's keenest appetite for wonder and amplification.

A THIRD instance may be thought still more remarkable.

" WE read perpetually of walls of fire raised by magical " art to stop the progress of knights-errant. In TASSO, the " wizard ISMENO guards the inchanted forest with walls of fire. " In the *Orlando Inamorato*, L. III. C. i. MANDRICARDO is " endeavoured to be stopped by enchanted flames ; but he

Thus far the learned editor of the *Fairy Queen* [Notes on B. III. c. xi. s. 25.] who contents himself, like a good Romance-critic, with observing the fact, without the irreverence of presuming to account for it. But if the profane will not be kept within this decent reserve, we may give them to understand, that this fancy, as wild as it appears, had some foundation in *truth*. For I make no question but these *fires*, raised by magical art, to stop the progress of assailants, were only the flames of FEUGREGEOIS, as it was called, that is of WILD-FIRE, which appeared so strange, on its first invention and application, in the barbarous ages.

WE hear much of its wonders in the history of the Crusades; and even so late as SPENSER's own time they were not forgotten. DAVILA, speaking of the siege of *Poitiers* in 1569, tells us——*Abbondavano nella citta le provisioni da guerra; tra le quali, quantita inestimabile di* FUOCHI ARTIFICIATI, *lavorati in diverse maniere, ne'quali avenano i defensori posta grandissima speranza di respingere gli assalti de'nemici.* Lib. v.

HENCE, without doubt, the *magical flames and fiery walls,* of the *Gothic* Romancers [g]; and who will say, that the *specious miracles* of HOMER himself had a better foundation ?

BUT, after all, this is not the sort of defence I mean chiefly to insist upon. Let others explain away these *wonders*, so offensive to certain philosophical critics. They are welcome to me in their own proper form, and with all the extravagance commonly imputed to them.

[g] For an account of some other wonders in Romance, such as *enchanted arms, invulnerable bodies, flying horses,* &c. see *L'Esprit des Loix,* l. xxviii. c. 22.

A P-

APPENDIX J.[1]

[1] A celebrated writer, whose good sense, or whose per-verseness, would not suffer him to be the dupe of French prejudices, declares himself roundly of this opinion : "On "a voulu mettre en *representation* (says he, speaking of the "absurd magnificence of the *French* Opera) le MERVEILLEUX, "qui, n'etant fait que pour être imaginé, EST AUSSI BIEN PLACE "DANS UN POEME EPIQUE que ridiculement sur un theatre." [*Nouv. Heloise*, p. II. l. xxiii.]

APPENDIX K.[2]

IT is, further, to be noted that the tale of *the Giant* OLYPHANT *and Chylde* TOPAZ was not a fiction of his own, but a story of antique fame, and very celebrated in the Days of Chivalry : so that nothing could better suit the poet's design of discrediting the old Romances, than the choice of this venerable legend for the vehicle of his ridicule upon them.

INDEED Sir TOPAZ is all Don QUIXOTE in little ; as you will easily see from comparing the two knights together ; who are drawn with the same features, are characterized by the same strokes, and differ from each other but as a sketch in miniature from a finished and full-sized picture.

1. CERVANTES is very particular in describing the *person* and *habit* of his Hero, agreeably to the known practice of the old Romancers. CHAUCER does the same by his knight, and in a manner that almost equals the arch-gravity of the *Spanish* author :

> Sir TOPAZ was a doughty swaine,
> White was his fàce as paine maine,
>   His lippes red as rose,
> His rudde is like scarlet in graine,
> And I you tell in good certaine,
>   *He had a seemely nose.*

> His haire, his berde, was like safroune,
> That to his girdle raught adowne,
>   His shoone of cordewaine,
> Of Bruges were his hosen broun,
> His robe was of chekelatoun,
>   That cost many a jane.

2. CERVANTES tells us how Don QUIXOTE passed his time in the country, before he turned Knight-errant. CHAUCER, in the same spirit, celebrates his knight's country diversions

of

of *hunting, hawking, shooting,* and *wrestling,* those known *prolusions* to feats of arms :

> He couth hunt at the wilde dere,
> And ride an bauking for by the rivere
>   With grey GOSHAUKE on honde,
> Thereto he was a good archere,
> Of wrastling was there none his pere
>   There any Ram should stonde.

3. THE Knights of Romance were used to dedicate their services to some paragon of beauty, such as was only conceived to exist in the land of Fairy, and could no where be found in this vulgar disenchanted world. Hence one of the strongest features in Don QUIXOTE's character is the sublime passion he had conceived for an imaginary or fairy mistress. Sir TOPAZ is not behind him in this extravagance :

> An Elfe-queene woll I love, I wis,
> For in this world no woman is
>   To be my make in towne,
> All other women I forsake
> And to an Elfe-queene I me take
>   By dale and eke by downe.

4. DON QUIXOTE's passion for this idol of his fancy was so violent, that, after all the bangs and bruises of the day, instead of suffering his weary limbs to take any rest, it occupied him all night with incessant dreams and reveries of his mistress. Sir TOPAZ is in the same woful plight :

> Sir TOPAZ eke so weary was—
> That down he laid him in that place—
> Oh, Saint MARY, benedicite
> What aileth this love at me
>   To blind me so sore ?

Me dreamed all this night parde
An Elfe-queen shall my leman be
. And sleepe under my gore.

5. As the chastity of the hero of LA MANCHA is well known, from a variety of trying temptations, so Sir TOPAZ distinguishes himself by this knightly virtue :

Full many a maide bright in boure
They mourne for him their paramoure.
Whan hem were bet to sleepe,
But he was chaste and no lechoure,
And sweet as is the bramble floure
That bereth the red hipe.

6. THE fight of Sir TOPAZ with the Giant of three heads, in honour of his mistress,

For needes must he fight
With a giant with heads thre,
For paramours and jolitie
Of one that shone full bright—

together with his arming, and the whole ridiculous preparation for the combat, described at large in several stanzas, is exactly in the style and taste of CERVANTES, on similar occasions.

7. CERVANTES gives us to understand that it was familiar with his knight to sleep in the open air, to endure all hardships that befell, and to let his horse graze by him. CHAUCER, in like manner, of his knight, with much humour :

And

> And for he was a knight auntrous,
> · He nolde slepen in none house
>   But liggen in his hood,
> His bright helme was his wanger
> And by him fed his destrer
>   Of herbes fine and good.

8. AND, lastly, as CERVANTES, after the example of the Romance-writers, will have it, that his knight surpasses all others of antient fame, so DAN CHAUCER is careful to vindicate this high prerogative, to his hero :

> Men speaken of Romances of pris
> Of HORNECHILD and of IPOTIS,
>   Of BEVIS and Sir GIE,
> Of Sir LIBEAUX and BLANDAMOURE ;
> But Sir TOPAZ, he beareth the floure
>   Of rial chivalrie."

THUS far, at least to this effect, the concealed author (for the dispensers of these fairy favours would not be inquired after) of this new interpretation of the *Rime of Sir* TOPAZ. Other circumstances of resemblance might be added (for when a well-grounded hint of this sort is once given, and opened in some instances, it is not difficult to pursue it), but one needs go no further to be certain that the general scope of this poem is, Burlesque.

ONLY, I would observe, that though, in this ridiculous ballad, the poet clearly intended to expose the Romances of the time, as they were commonly written, he did not

the serious air, and very different conduct, of the SQUIRE's TALE; which SPENSER and MILTON were so particularly pleased with.

WE learn too, from the same tale, that, though CHAUCER could be as pleasant on the other fooleries of Romance, as any modern critic, he let the *marvellous* of it escape his ridicule, or rather esteemed this character of the *Gothic* Romance, no foolery. For the tale of CAMBUSCAN is all over MARVELLOUS; and MILTON, by specifying the *virtuous ring and glass*, and *the wondrous horse of brass*, as the circumstances that charmed him most, shews very plainly, that, in his opinion, these amusing fictions were well placed, and of principal consideration, as they surely are, in this *Fairy way of writing.*

BUT, whatever our old Bard would insinuate by his management of this enchanting tale, and whatever conclusions have, in fact, been drawn from it by such superior and congenial spirits as our two epic poets, the *half-told* story of CAMBUSCAN could never atone for the mischiefs done to the cause of Romance, by the pointed ridicule of *the Rime of Sir* TOPAZ. Common readers would be naturally induced by it to reject the old Romances, in the gross: and thus it happened, according to the observation I set out with, "that these "phantoms of Chivalry had the misfortune to be laughed "out of countenance by men of sense, before the substance "of it had been fairly and truly represented by any capable "writer."

PLEASE DO NOT REMOVE
CARDS OR SLIPS FROM THIS POCKET

UNIVERSITY OF TORONTO LIBRARY

PR   Hurd, Richard, Bp. of
3517   Worcester
H78A16   Hurd's letters on chivalry

CPSIA information can be obtained
at www.ICGtesting.com
Printed in the USA
BVOW06s2251170917
495139BV00017B/238/P